ArtScroll Series®

Rabbi Nosson Scherman / Rabbi Meir Zlotowitz

General Editors

RABBI YISSOCHER FRAND

Published by

Mesorah Publications, ltd

IN PRINT

Contemporary and Classic Issues
Through the Prism of Torah

written in collaboration with
Yonoson Rosenblum

FIRST EDITION
First Impression . . . September, 1995

Published and Distributed by
MESORAH PUBLICATIONS, Ltd.
4401 Second Avenue
Brooklyn, New York 11232

Distributed in Europe by
J. LEHMANN HEBREW BOOKSELLERS
20 Cambridge Terrace
Gateshead, Tyne and Wear
England NE8 1RP

Distributed in Israel by
SIFRIATI / A. GITLER — BOOKS
4 Bilu Street
P.O.B. 14075
Tel Aviv 61140

Distributed in Australia & New Zealand by
GOLDS BOOK & GIFT CO.
36 William Street
Balaclava 3183, Vic., Australia

Distributed in South Africa by
KOLLEL BOOKSHOP
22 Muller Street
Yeoville 2198, Johannesburg, South Africa

ISBN:
0-89906-630-5 (hard cover)
0-89906-631-3 (paperback)

Typography by CompuScribe at ArtScroll Studios, Ltd.
4401 Second Avenue / Brooklyn, N.Y. 11232 / (718) 921-9000

Printed in the United States of America by Noble Book Press Corp.
Bound by Sefercraft Quality Bookbinders, Ltd., Brooklyn, N.Y.

The author dedicates this book to his mother,

Mrs. Adele Frand

חיה ברכה בת אסתר שתחי׳

She has always been

and continues to be an inspiration,

a source of strength and faith,

and a model of the Jewish mother.

May the z'chus of this volume

help bring her

to a complete and speedy recovery

from her recent illness

and may she merit many more years

of fruitful activity

on behalf of all who know and love her.

מכתב ברכה

Rabbi Yaakov S. Weinberg
400 Mt. Wilson Lane • Baltimore, MD 21208

Ner Israel Rabbinical College
Rosh Hayeshiva

ישיבת נר ישראל
ראש הישיבה

אך למותר לתאר גדול חשיבות שיחות התורה של הרה״ג
המופלג הרב יששכר דוב פראנד שליט״א המבארות הלכות
מסובכות והשקפות נחוצות ביסודי הדת ועקרי התורה בכשרון
נפלא ובלשון מושכל המתקבל על הלב. וכבר קנו דיבוריו מקום
נכבד ברחבי עולם התורה ויפוצו מעייונתיו חוצה. ואפריון
נמטייה לחברת ארטסקרול שהשכילו לעשות בהדפסת דבריו
למען ירחיבו גבול הנהנים מתורתו כי טוב.

הכותב לכבוד המחבר ותורתו,

מכתב ברכה

ישיבה דפילאדעלפיא
TALMUDICAL YESHIVA OF PHILADELPHIA

6063 Drexel Road
Philadelphia, Pennsylvania 19131
215 - 477 - 1000

בס״ד

ד׳ לחדש אני לדודי קדוש השם לפ״ק

למע״כ ידידי היקר הרה״ג מרביץ תורה לרבים
וכו׳ וכו׳ ר׳ יששכר דוב פראנד שליט״א ר״מ
בישיבה הק׳ נר ישראל באלטימאר

אחרי דרך מבוא השלו׳ והברכה.

שמחתי באומרים שהמוסד מסורה ארטסקרול מוכן להדפיס
את הקסטות התורניות שכב׳ הרצה. הם דברים נחמדים וחריפים
וכבר נתפרסמו לטובה ועושים רושם גדול על שומעיהם. אשרי
לו שזכה לזכות את הרבים בדבריו הנלבבים. בטוח שדברים
היוצאים מלבו עושים רושם על כל שומע.

ברור שעל ידי שידפיסו הקסטות תתרבה ההזדמנות לעורר
ולחזק מבקשי האמת ויראי השי״ת. יישר חילם של המוסד
מסורה ארטסקרול שעל ידם מתרבה לימוד התורה בישראל.
בברכת חו״ש והצלחה אמיתית כתיבה וחתימה טובה.

בידידות כנה

שמואל קמנצקי

Table of Contents

Contemporary Issues

Timeless Topics

Author's Preface

I.

In the sixteen pieces that comprise this book, I have attempted to restate time-honored Torah principles as they relate to pressing contemporary issues in a manner that people can relate to. To borrow from the famous introduction to *Mesillas Yesharim*:

I have written this work ... to remind [men] of what they already know ... for you will find in most of my words only things that most people know and concerning which they entertain no doubts. But to the extent that they are well known ... so are they commonly ignored and forget-fulness in relation to them is prevalent.

If there is anything new here it is only in the application of eternal truths to modern circumstances.

These essays are drawn from *drashos* delivered over a period of ten years. It is my hope that these words will be read in the spirit in which they were originally delivered — as conversations with myself. Reading them over again, I recall in many cases the personal issues with which I was grappling that inspired them. Though I have written about controlling anger and *chinuch habanim,* for instance, I am far from being an expert or a paragon of virtue in these areas, or with respect to any other *middah* discussed in this book. It is my own sense of human frailty in these areas that triggered these internal dialogues in the first place.

II.

This book, like many of the most rewarding aspects of my life, has come about not through any process of careful planning on my part. As has happened so many times in the past, I am once again forced to recognize that the best things in life come as a consequence of Hashem's plans, and not ours.

Twenty years ago, the suggestion was made that I start a *chaburah* in Yeshivas Ner Yisrael devoted to learning those *masechtos* (tractates) that readily lend themselves to *halachah le'ma'aseh.* My initial reaction was one of extreme skepticism that such a project could succeed in the Yeshiva. But twelve intrepid pioneers agreed to risk their afternoon *seder,* and the *chaburah* began. That original *chaburah* has since grown into a regular *shiur* in the Yeshiva. No one — and certainly not myself — could have anticipated that this *shiur* would flourish despite the lack of strategic planning or clear precedent.

Some years later, a friend suggested that I give a *shiur* on halachic issues stemming from the weekly Torah reading. We began with no more than a *minyan* in a third-floor attic of the Agudath Israel of Baltimore. I remember thinking at the time that if there was not sufficient interest I would simply stop for the summer and not resume in the fall. More than a dozen years later, it is hard to imagine my life without that Thursday night *shiur*. Once again, that *shiur* became part of my life without any advance planning on my part.

As the Thursday night *shiur* grew, it was suggested that I tape the *drashos* for widespread dissemination. The technical and logistical aspects of such an undertaking were daunting, and the skeptic in me held out little hope that there would be widespread interest. But once again I was proven wrong.

This book follows the same pattern. Again the idea came not from me but from several friends who saw in the *drashos* potential for a book. And again, I was skeptical. There is a vast difference between the spoken and written word, and I doubted my ability to bridge that gap. I hope, however, that once again my doubts will prove unjustified, and that Hashem, Who has granted me the *zechus* to disseminate His Torah in Baltimore and beyond, will grant me that privilege once more.

III.

A Jew has a source of guidance for every moment of his life: the Torah. The Torah teaches us how to rejoice, and how, G-d forbid, to mourn. From the manner in which the *bikkurim* (first-fruit offerings) were brought up to Yerushalayim, we also learn how to give thanks to Hashem for His bounty. We thank Hashem not only for the gift of the fruits themselves but for everything He has done for us that enabled us to reach that moment. (See *Alshich* to *Ki Savo*.)

Therefore let me begin by thanking my parents: my late father, Mr. David Frand *a"h*, and my mother, may she live and be well,

Mrs. Adele Frand. My parents made many sacrifices to raise me as an Orthodox Jew in what was a small Jewish community of Seattle, Washington more than 40 years ago. Chief among those sacrifices was sending me away as a young boy across the continent to learn in Yeshivas Ner Yisrael in Baltimore, despite the fact that air travel was much less common than today and our separations were for many months at a time.

My wife's mother, Rebbetzin Esther Blumenkrantz, has been more like a mother than a mother-in-law to me. Her greatest source of joy has been to see her children and grandchildren involved in Torah. Unfortunately my wife's father, Rabbi Jacob Blumenkrantz zt"l, passed away before our marriage and I was not able to benefit directly from his vast storehouse of Torah knowledge and wisdom.

My dear children Yaakov, Avigayil, and Baruch deserve my gratitude for having graciously allowed themselves to be mentioned as subjects of many of my stories and, as a result, to "suffer" some good-natured ribbing by their peers.

Yeshivas Ner Yisrael, which became a second home for me over 30 years ago, remains my home today. I truly give thanks to the *Ribbono Shel Olam* for granting me my portion among those who sit in the *beis hamedrash*. I owe an unpayable debt to the entire *hanhalah* of the Yeshiva for all the efforts they invested in me. The closeness I developed with my Rosh Hayeshiva, HaRav HaGaon Rabbi Yaakov Yitzchok Ruderman *zt"l*, allowed me to observe a *gadol b'Torah* (Torah giant) close up. The present Rosh Hayeshiva, HaRav HaGaon Rabbi Yaakov Weinberg *shlita*, has been instrumental in my growth in learning and *hashkafah*. I feel privileged to call HaRav Naftali Neuberger *shlita*, my *rebbi* in *chochmas hachaim* (wisdom of the world). I would like to single out two *rebbeim* who had a profound impact on me, as they did on hundreds of other *talmidim*. They are: the saintly *Mashgiach* of the Yeshiva,

HaRav HaGaon Rabbi Dovid Kronglass *z"tl*, and *ye'bodail l'chaim*, HaRav HaGaon Rabbi Yakov Moshe Kulefsky *shlita*. It would take an entire chapter to thank all the *chaverim* (friends) who have had a profound impact on me over the years and whose insights are reflected throughout the book.

The tapes from which these essays were drawn are distributed by the Yad Yechiel Institute, and I would like to thank the three individuals whose initiative, toil, and resources brought the Yad Yechiel Institute into being: Dr. Marcel Reischer, in whose father's name the institute was endowed; Mr. Joseph Pollock; and Mrs. Laure Gutman. May the *Ribbono Shel Olam* repay them for all their efforts and kindnesses.

When the history of Torah Judaism in America is written, a chapter will surely be devoted to ArtScroll/Mesorah Publications, which, under the guidance of Rabbis Meir Zlotowitz and Nosson Scherman, has made an indelible impact on the study of Torah in the English-speaking world. In addition to Rabbis Zlotowitz and Scherman, I am grateful to Mr. Shmuel Blitz, director of ArtScroll's Israeli operations, for having made the *shidduch* with Rabbi Yonoson Rosenblum, and to Rabbi Avrohom Biderman, with whom I have worked closely on this project. I also appreciate the dedicated efforts of the other members of the ArtScroll/Mesorah staff: Reb Eli Kroen who produced the striking cover design, Mrs. Devory Bick, Toby Brander, and Udi Hershkowitz who worked on the book's many revisions, Rochel Leah Ross who did the typesetting, Fayge Silverman who read the manuscript and offered her insights, and Mrs. Faygie Weinbaum and Mrs. Mindy Stern who proofread and commented.

IV.

Lastly I must thank two people without whom this project would never have come to fruition.

Writing talent is a gift from Hashem. Just as most of us are inspired, sometimes awed, by a beautiful voice, we can also be inspired by an eloquent pen. Rabbi Yonoson Rosenblum, who collaborated with me in the writing of this book, possesses such a gift. I am grateful to him for the way in which he preserved the spirit of the original *drashos* in writing, a task that would have been beyond the capacity of many fine writers. Reb Yonoson acted as an editor as well, offering a number of insights and suggestions that improved upon the original *drashos*.

A number of years ago, I received a letter from HaRav HaGaon Rabbi Mordechai Gifter *shlita*, who had taken the time to comment on an article of mine in *The Jewish Observer*. He added to his words of encouragement, this piece of advice: "Always speak in impeccable English. It is a *kavod Shomayim*." I will not claim to have always done so, but having Reb Yonoson help me with this book has helped me come closer to fulfilling Rabbi Gifter's charge.

My wife Nechama has not only been the editor for all my speeches and articles, as well as for this book; she has been my editor in life. Her editor's keen sense of what can and should be said, when it should be said, and how it should be said, has been my constant guide. Her wise counsel, her insights into life's mysteries, her perspective, help, and encouragement, and, yes, her criticism have made her an *ezer kenegdo* in the fullest sense (see *Netziv* to Bereishis 2:18). In the immortal words of Rabbi Akiva: *Sheli veshelochem shelah hi*.

Our Sages tell us that we must offer thanks to *HaKadosh Baruch Hu* for all his past kindnesses and beseech His continued help for the future. I am truly humbled by all the goodness He has showered upon me — *Katonti mekol hachassidim* — and pray for His continued *chesed* in all my endeavors and that my wife and I should continue to reap much *nachas* from the wonderful children with whom we have been blessed.

Yissocher Frand
Menachem Av, 5755
Baltimore, MD.

RABBI YISSOCHER FRAND

IN PRINT

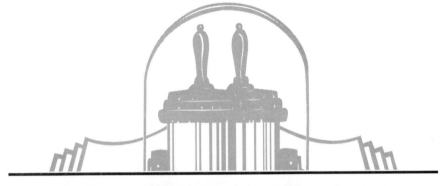

TESHUVAH

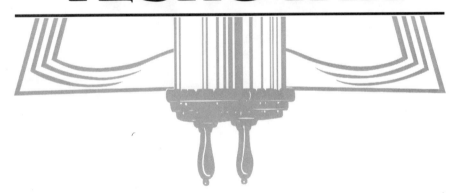

Teshuvah: Knowing Ourselves and Who We Could Be

The Gerrer Rebbe once met a young man learning at Ohr Somayach in Jerusalem, and asked him where he learned. The young man replied that he learned at Ohr Somayach, but hastened to add, "But I am not a *ba'al teshuvah*." The Rebbe did not hesitate before asking him, "*Farvost nit* — Why not?"

The Gerrer Rebbe's question is one that we have to confront on a constant basis, and in particular as we approach the *Yomim Noraim* (the Days of Awe).

Teshuvah (repentance) is not something done on the spur of the moment; it is a process in stages. The verse (Eichah 3:40), in fact, describes *teshuvah* as the culmination of a three-step process: 'נחפשה דרכינו ונחקרה ונשובה עד ה. First we must examine our ways, then we must search ourselves, engage in a process of deep introspection, and only then are we ready to return to Hashem.

Part of our problem in answering the Gerrer Rebbe's question is that we are often stuck at the first stage of the process. When we examine our ways, we are pretty satisfied with what we find. We are *shomrei Shabbos,* we keep *kashrus,* we have a fixed daily schedule of learning. What more could Hashem want from us?

And indeed there is some basis to our self-evaluations, especially if we compare ourselves to the broader Jewish world. But at the same time, we should not be too hasty in measuring ourselves for one of the seats closest to the *Kisei HaKavod* (the Divine throne).

To know why not, let us examine the *parashah* of *vidui ma'aseros* (the confession recited together with the bringing of the *ma'aser* tithes). At first glance, the term *vidui* (confession) applied to this recitation is problematic. Generally we think of *vidui* in terms of the thumping of our chests during the *Al Chaits* on Yom Kippur and the repetition of חטאתי עייתי, פשעתי. But in *vidui ma'aser* there is seemingly no mention of our having sinned or having done anything wrong. Quite the contrary. What we "confess" is that we have given all the tithes that we were supposed to: "I have removed the holy things from the house, and I have also given to the Levi, to the proselyte, to the orphan, and to the widow, according (ככל) to whatever commandment You have commanded me..." (Devarim 26:13).

But hidden in this recitation, say the commentators, is one tiny letter, כ, which is a form of confession. For we do not say that we have given everything precisely as commanded but rather *like all* (ככל) that we were commanded. Yes, we gave the tithes, but perhaps not in the optimal fashion. We waited until the end of three years to dispense them rather than giving each one in its proper year.

And herein lies the lesson for us. If we examine our deeds, we will see that the form of all the mitzvos is there, but often there is something lacking in the content. We avoid any of the prohibited activities on Shabbos, but is our Shabbos table truly *Shabbosdik*? Is it given over exclusively to *divrei Torah* and *zemiros* and allowing the children to share what they learned during the week? Or is it a place for the discussion of *shul* politics, a critique of the performance of the *ba'al kriah,* or the fate of the local gridiron heroes?

Sure we *daven,* but do we always make an effort to *daven* with a *minyan?* Or is our *Shacharis* fifteen minutes grabbed before the morning car pool, our *Minchah* five minutes behind a closed door in the office rather than in the downtown *minyan,* and our *Ma'ariv* again in the house before going to sleep?

There is a commandment of פרו ורבו. The first term, says Rabbi Samson Raphael Hirsch, refers to the mitzvah of having children; the second to the mitzvah of guiding them towards a certain goal in life, as an archer shoots (רובה) an arrow towards the target. And we have to ask ourselves: Are we fulfilling the second part of the mitzvah? Do we spend time with our children? Play with them? Do we learn with them on Shabbos or do we count the minutes until we can send them to a Pirchei group so that we can spend the rest of Shabbos sleeping?

I am not going to go through every mitzvah in the Torah and a litany of ways in which we fall short in our performance of them. Each of us, if we make a careful examination of our ways, will be able to find areas in need of improvement. The point is to remember the כ modifying כל in the *vidui ma'aser* so that we are not left with the pleasant, but ultimately damaging, conclusion that perfection is just around the corner.

Identifying concrete ways in which we can improve our mitzvah observance is, however, only the first stage of the *teshuvah* process, and not the most difficult. The next stage is one of deep introspection to identify our true potential and the nature of the unique task for which Hashem brought us into the world.

On Rosh Hashanah, *Adam HaRishon* was created and on that same day he was judged. That judgment consisted of a single word — איכה — usually translated as "where are you?," but encompassing much, much more. With that one sin Adam had changed the course of all history, and this is suggested in Hashem's question: איכה. *Chazal* tell us that Hashem's question hinted to the unlimited potential that had been lost: "Yesterday you reached until the Heavens, encompassing the entire world from one end to the other. You were the work of My hands, My special creation. And where are you today? Hiding among the trees of the garden."

The second stage of *teshuvah* — נחקרה — demands of us that we ask ourselves: What is my potential? Where has it gone? What am I using it for? The word איכה calls out to each Jew to recognize that he has a unique mission in this world, which he must discover for himself.

Adam HaRishon's tragedy was the failure to realize his vast potential. Avraham *Avinu's* triumph was that he did. *Akeidas Yitzchak* (the Binding of Isaac) occurred when Avraham was already 137 years old. By that time, Avraham had introduced monotheism to the world; he and Sarah had brought many under the *kanfei haShechinah* (the wings of the Divine Presence); he stood on one side while all the rest of the world stood on the other, and by so doing revolutionized human society; he had been thrown into a fiery furnace and emerged unscathed; he had been tested nine times by Hashem and prevailed in each of those tests.

And yet Avraham had still not reached his full potential nor had he stopped striving. Without the tenth and final test, without the command to kill his son, his only son from Sarah, the son whom he loved and in whom all his hopes were placed, Avraham would not have realized all the potential with which he was brought down to the world. Only as he raised the knife to slaughter Yitzchak was his life's mission complete. At that moment, the angel called out, "Avraham, Avraham," and the *Yalkut Shimoni* comments that the reference is to the two Avrahams — the one who exists as potential in Heaven and the one who exists in this world. At that moment, the two Avrahams were perfectly congruent; at 137 years of age, Avraham had achieved the goal for which we were all created — that of bringing the Avraham below into conformity with the ideal Avraham above.

Before we are created, the *Ribbono shel Olam* has a clear image of who we can be and what our mission in life is. That image remains always in Heaven. It was Avraham's unique achievement to fulfill that image, but the task of doing so is imposed equally on each and every one of us. There is a beautiful story about the *Netziv* of Volozhin that illustrates this point. As a young boy, the *Netziv* did not apply himself in his studies and there were no great expectations for him. When he was about nine years old, he overheard his parents discussing his future. His despairing father cried that nothing he had tried — prizes, private tutors — seemed to have had any effect. Finally, the *Netziv's* father and mother concluded that there was no choice but to apprentice him to a shoemaker or tailor. Hearing his parents' plans, the young boy was overcome with remorse. He rushed into the room where his parents were talking and promised that from then on he would apply himself with rigor to his studies.

The rest, as they say, is history. The *Netziv* wrote voluminously and many of his works are classics — *Haamek Davar* on *Chumash, Haamek She'alah* on the *Shiltos* of Rav Achai

Gaon, his collected responsa *Meishiv Davar*, and *Meromei Sadeh*. He was the Rosh Yeshiva of the Volozhin Yeshiva, the preeminent yeshiva of his time and the progenitor of all subsequent Lithuanian yeshivos. I remember my Rosh Yeshiva, Rabbi Yaakov Yitzchak Ruderman, once mentioning a difficulty posed by the *Netziv* in a *shiur*. The question posed sounded strange to us, and a number of the *talmidim* laughed. With that Rabbi Ruderman got angry. "You are laughing at a difficulty posed by the *Netziv*," he shouted. "There is not one of you who, if he learned day and night for the next hundred years, would approach the ankles of the *Netziv*, and you dare to laugh."

In any event, when the *Netziv* completed *Haamek She'alah*, he made a *seudas hoda'ah* (a meal of thanksgiving to Hashem) that he had merited to finish the work. With tears in his eyes, the *Netziv* related why the occasion was such a personal celebration for him. He told the story of overhearing his parents discussing his future, and went on to describe the course his life would have taken had his father gone ahead with his plan to apprentice him to a craftsman.

> *I would have been a fine layman. Erev Yom Kippur I would have thought to myself, "I do my work honestly; I don't cheat anyone; I'm an erlicher Yid (upright Jew)." After 120 years I would have gotten to Shomayim (Heaven), and they would have asked me, "Where is Haamek Davar, where is the Meishiv Davar, where is the Haamek She'alah?"*
>
> *I would have thought they were crazy. "What do you mean? I'm a poshuter (simple) shoemaker, an am ha'aretz (an unlearned person). Why are you asking me why I did not write great works of scholarship?"*

The *Netziv* was describing the huge gap that can exist between the Heavenly image that precedes our birth and one's actual accomplishments. Who knows how many shoemakers were supposed to bequeath to the world great works of Torah scholarship? More importantly, for our purposes, who knows how far we are from fulfilling the mission for which we were created?

Yet even after hearing the story of the *Netziv,* most of us may easily conclude that *we* were certainly not formed for such intellectual achievements — that Rabbi Ruderman was right when he said that even if we learned day and night for a hundred years we would not touch the *Netziv.* And quite possibly we were not fashioned to be another *Netziv.* But could we at least be a Reb Dovid Dryan?

Who, you will ask, was Reb Dovid Dryan? He was a *talmid* of the *Chafetz Chaim,* who was so influenced by the *Chafetz Chaim* that his whole life he spoke only in half sentences so as to be as careful as possible in speech. Reb Dovid was not a great *talmid chacham.* After Radin, his learning was largely confined to *Mishnayos* and *Chumash.* Eventually he became a *shochet* in Gateshead, England. Soon after his arrival, he realized that there was no yeshiva in Gateshead, and he decided that he could not live or raise his family in a city without a yeshiva. So he wrote to the *Chafetz Chaim* and asked him to send a *rosh yeshiva* to this tiny backwater in northern England, at a time when all of Western Europe probably did not have a handful of yeshivos.

The *Chafetz Chaim* complied and sent a *rosh yeshiva.* Next Reb Dovid traveled to London and started rounding up students for his yeshiva one at a time. Then he decided to bring a *kollel* to Gateshead, and persuaded Rabbi Eliyahu Dessler to spend a few days a week in Gateshead to supervise the *kollel.* Rabbi Dessler also became the inspiration and guide for Mr. and Mrs. Avrohom Kohn, who founded the great Gateshead Seminary. Over the years, Gateshead became the most important center of Torah learning in Europe, and only because of one layman who said, "I cannot live in a place without a yeshiva."

When Rabbi Shneur Kotler heard this story, he commented that had Reb Dovid Dryan never founded Gateshead, he would no doubt have arrived in *Gan Eden* feeling that he had lived up to his obligations on earth. After all, his *chalaf* (knife for ritual slaughtering) was always kosher and he never spoke *lashon hara*. How surprised he would have been to be asked why he, a simple *shochet,* did not build a major Torah center.

Reb Shraga Feivel Mendlowitz was a highly original thinker with broad knowledge in almost every area of Torah. Among the subjects that he taught was *tefillah* (prayer). One year before Rosh Hashanah, he was going through the section of the *Amidah* known as *Zichronos*, in which each person is described as being judged according to his מעשיו ופקדתו. The first term, מעשיו, he explained, means his deeds. But what, then, can the second term, פקדתו, mean, for how else is a man judged other than by his deeds? Reb Shraga Feivel explained פקדתו to mean a person's purpose in life. In other words, we are judged not only by the quality of our deeds but to the extent to which we fulfill our unique purpose in life.

When he said this, Reb Shraga Feivel continued, "How can a person know whether he has fulfilled his purpose?" and broke down crying. Here was someone who had built Torah Vodaath, the first major yeshiva in America, and founded Torah Umesorah, which spearheaded the whole day school movement in America — a man whose impact on the development of Orthodox Jewry in America was second to none. Yet he felt no assurance that he had reached his potential, that he had brought the heavenly Reb Shraga Feivel to earth.

We live in a society in which people are pretty much put out to pasture at the age of 65 when they start collecting social security. Hopefully they have saved enough for a condominium in Florida where they can enjoy the rest of their lives in sunshine. But for us it's not like that. The process of trying to reach our potential is a never-ending one. We are in the same boat as our forefather Avraham, who was still being put to the most difficult test any human being could ever face at 137.

In his last years, when he was old and frail, Rabbi Ruderman once bemoaned the fact that he did not feel he was achieving in his later years. He admitted that in his younger years he had achieved something, without mentioning finishing all of *Shas* as a teenager, writing *Avodas HaLevi* while still in his early 20s, and founding Ner Israel Yeshiva. But that still did not give him peace of mind that nothing more was demanded of him. His only consolation as his strength waned was that he was personally supporting and supervising a *ba'al teshuvah,* whose family had cut him off. The point here is the intensity with which someone who had done so much still felt the need to find a purpose in his life.

Still we might say to ourselves: True, there was more I could have done and perhaps I did not use my abilities to the fullest, but surely I will be judged first and foremost by whether I observed the mitzvos.

There is a famous story in *Melachim* involving the wicked King Achav and Navos. Navos owned a vineyard adjacent to Achav's palace, and Achav decided that he just had to have that vineyard. Navos refused to sell. Achav's wife Jezebel was even more evil than he, and she hired two witnesses to perjure themselves that Navos had committed a capital offense. As a consequence, Navos was put to death, and Achav seized his field.

Yalkut Shimoni asks why Navos, who did nothing more than refuse to part with the portion of land allocated to him by Hashem, met such a tragic fate. And here the *Yalkut* gives a truly frightening answer. We are commanded to honor Hashem with those abilities and talents with which he has favored us, the *Yalkut* says. Navos had an extremely beautiful voice. When he came to Jerusalem on the festivals, Jews flocked to hear him *daven* and were uplifted by his *davening*. Once, however, Navos did not feel like being the *shaliach tzibbur* and refused to *daven*. For no reason other than personal convenience he deprived multitudes from being elevated in their service of God. For that refusal, the *Midrash* concludes, he met such a horrible end.

Obviously Navos was a *tzaddik*. Otherwise he would not have refused Achav's offer of a generous price for his vineyard. Nevertheless he suffered an unhappy end because he refused — even once — to use the powers that *Hakadosh Baruch Hu* had given him.

⌁ WHY ME — WHY NOW?

Every *Amidah* of Yom Kippur ends with a strange phrase: "My G-d, before I was formed I was unworthy, and now that I have been formed, it is as if I had not been formed." Rabbi Avraham Yitzchak Kook interpreted this sentence as follows:

> *Until I was born, it was not the time for me; my specific mission in life was for this period and no other. And now that I have come into this historical epoch, it is as if I was never born, for I have squandered the abilities that were given me in order to fulfill this mission.*

Not only is each one of us brought into the world with a unique combination of strengths, but each of us is brought into the world at a particular time when those powers are needed for the fulfillment of some part of the Divine plan. Thus נחקרה requires both introspection concerning ourselves and intense reflection concerning the situation of the Jewish people in the period in which we live.

If one reads interviews with survivors of terrible tragedies, they all have a common thread running through them. The survivors feel that their survival places upon them a certain responsibility, that there must have been some reason why they were spared. Many emerge with a feeling that they must dedicate their lives to some higher purpose.

As observant Jews living in the last decades of the twentieth century, we are all survivors of an unparalleled tragedy, and we continue to be survivors of the wholesale assimilation of American Jewry. Whether or not our parents or grandparents escaped from the furnace themselves, each of us is the culmination of a long historical process during which our ranks have been continually weeded by oppressors great and small. And we, the surviving remnant, have to ask ourselves, for what purpose were we chosen?

Reb Yosef Rosenberger can serve as an exemplar for us of what it means to take to heart the significance of one's personal salvation. Along with a large number of other Viennese Jews he was sent to Dachau shortly after the Nazi *Anschluss* (annexation of Austria). He, however, was one of the lucky ones. After several months, he was released from Dachau. In his case, the time in Dachau probably saved his life. His affidavit of financial support from an American sponsor was not a "strong" one, and only the fact that the American consul in Vienna took pity on him because of his experiences allowed him to obtain a visa.

Shortly after his arrival in America, another Jew from Vienna, who knew that Reb Yosef's parents had owned a clothing store, asked him how one could be sure that garments bought in America did not contain the halachically prohibited blend of wool and linen. Reb Yosef did not know, and when he tried to find out, he learned that the prohibition on wearing wool and linen garments was almost entirely ignored in America. Neither tailors nor laymen knew much about it. Even those aware of the prohibition assumed that linen was no longer used in modern clothing manufacture.

Reb Yosef had to ask himself: Why me? Why had he been one of the fortunate ones who managed to leave Vienna in time, and why had he been asked about *shatnez*? He concluded that he had been chosen to return the mitzvah of *shatnez* back to its proper place in Jewish life. From then on, he was a man with a mission. Over the next year, he enrolled in a special textile high school, worked menial jobs in the garment industry, and haunted the New York Public Library reading scholarly tomes on linen in an effort to develop a quick, accurate, and inexpensive test for the presence of linen. Even when that was achieved he still had to make a largely apathetic public aware of the problem. Every minute of his day and nearly every penny he had was devoted to this effort. It was years before he had saved enough money not be laughed at when he sought a marriage partner.

But because of his single-minded determination, a prohibition once ignored by 90 percent of the *shomer Shabbos* Jews in America is today almost universally observed. Hundreds, if not thousands, of *shatnez* checkers around the world have been personally trained by Reb Yosef or by those trained by him. And Mr. Rosenberger, now well into his eighties, still personally checks ten thousand garments a year for a standard fee of only two dollars a garment.

◄ INTROSPECTION AND THE YOM KIPPUR DAVENING

If we took seriously the need to think deeply about ourselves in order to ascertain what unique task, in this particular time, has been placed upon us, we would sit down with our spouses, a friend, or our *rav* and talk these issues out. The likelihood, however, is that we will put off as long as possible the questions: Who am I? Where am I going? Am I using the abilities that Hashem gave me for the purposes he intended? On Yom Kippur, we will dutifully confess our various transgressions and resolve once again to speak less *lashon hara* in the coming year, to count to ten before expressing anger, etc. But we must remember to ask ourselves *the* question — איכה — Where are you?

Yet the Yom Kippur *davening* itself forces us to confront this question. As the day wanes and the gates of repentance are closing shut, it is precisely this question which is thrust upon us. At *Minchah* we read the story of Yonah. On one level, of course, Yonah is a powerful reminder of the power of *teshuvah*. On another level, however, Yonah is the classic story of one who tried to flee from the task which Hashem had assigned him. Yonah fled to Tarshish, then to the sea, then to the hold of the ship, and finally to his private world of dreams. But wherever he went Hashem pursued him. He could not escape his appointed destiny.

Chazal wanted us to confront the Yonah within us in these last hours of Yom Kippur, when our lives are hanging in the balance. Yes, you regret the *lashon hara* and the time wasted from *Torah* study, *Sefer Yonah* says to us, but that is only part of the process. Identify your destiny and resolve to face it rather than flee from it, for to flee from it is the path toward oblivion.

With that message in mind, we are now ready for *Ne'ilah*, the closing prayer, the two most precious hours of the year. Like a marathon runner with the finish line only a mile away, we reach down for the last bit of strength, for the courage to confront the question: איכה. Just when we finally feel ready for a complete *teshuvah* and feel ready to go through the *al chaits* again with increased fervor, we discover there are no more *al chaits*. Repentance on individual sins is no longer the issue.

Instead of the *al chait,* we say to the *Ribbono shel Olam,* "You have taught us, Hashem, our G-d, to confess before You regarding all our sins in order that we can withdraw our hands from all that we have taken wrongfully." There is no mitzvah of *teshuvah* written explicitly in the Torah, just a mitzvah of confession, which is written in the *parashah* dealing with theft. And the ultimate theft, writes the *Chiddushei HaRim,* is that which we steal from Hashem when we do not use the powers He gave us for the purposes He intended. We confess at the end of *Ne'ilah* our misappropriation of our G-d-given talents. "All that was taken wrongfully" is that which we took from Hashem and did not consecrate to His purposes.

Now we are finally at the third stage of "נשובה אליך" — we

will return to You," which, says Rav Zadok, means dedicating all our strength to Hashem's service. We know repentance is possible because "[Hashem's] right hand is outstretched to receive those who return," just as a loving father reaches out to his wayward children. The father may become impatient or angry, but in the end he forgives them: "They are good children; they have such great strengths; they want to live up to their potential."

And we in turn must dare to be great; dare to find out who we really are and for what purpose Hashem created us.

Step by Step, Moment by Moment

Many of us are last-minute shoppers when it comes to doing *teshuvah*. At one time, Jews started the intense *teshuvah* process with the first sound of the *shofar* on *Rosh Chodesh Elul*. Anyone who had the privilege of seeing my *Rosh HaYeshiva* Rabbi Yaakov Yitzchak Ruderman or the *Mashgiach* Rabbi Dovid Kronglass in *Elul* could see on their faces that this was a different month. Such people, unfortunately, are few and far between today. The rest of us usually do not focus our energies on the task at hand until some time between the beginning of *Selichos* and *Erev Rosh Hashanah*.

When we finally do sit down to make the *cheshbon hanefesh*, the spiritual account-taking that must precede any meaningful *teshuvah*, we are like businessmen toting up the end of the year profits and losses. For some of us, the end of the year comes with a great sense of relief: We realize that the year has not been a good one and look forward to the opportunity, we hope, to open up a new balance sheet. If we are in that category, we can appreciate the words of the *Gemara* in *Megillah* referring to the fact that the last Torah reading of the year is always *Nitzavim*, with its terrible curses. "Let the year and its curses end," says the *Gemara*, "so that the new one and its blessings may begin."

For some, the end of the year accounting may even bring on thoughts that are close to blasphemous. They may say to themselves that they did, in fact, improve, but Hashem did not respond to that improvement as they had anticipated. It is perhaps to wipe all such thoughts from our mind that we begin our *Selichos* with the following preamble: "To You, Hashem, is the righteousness, and to us the humiliation." In effect, we are reminding ourselves that *teshuvah* can only take place when we first acknowledge that Hashem's judgment is just, whether we comprehend it or not. The Kotzker *Rebbe's* entire *Selichos* consisted of this one sentence. He would come to *shul* on *Motzaei Shabbos* for the first night of *Selichos*, recite this verse, and leave. For him, nothing more need be said.

Indeed, when we consider the year past and think to ourselves, "It's the same old story — the same sins as last year, the same lack of noticeable improvement," our natural reaction is to be shamefaced. And when we look in the *Rambam's Hilchos Teshuvah* for some help with the *teshuvah* process, our despair may only increase. There we find in the second chapter the *Rambam's* definition of a true *ba'al teshuvah*: one upon whom

Hashem Himself can bear witness that he will not repeat his previous sin again. That is a daunting standard to live up to, especially when each of us recognizes how many times we have repeated sins for which we felt intense regret and shame.

Our situation is much like that of Adam, the first man. After his sin, he told Hashem, "The woman that You gave to be with me — she gave me to eat of the tree, and I will eat" (Bereishis 3:12). The commentators are puzzled by Adam's use of the future tense — "I will eat." Why did he not say, "And I ate?" It sounds like the height of *chutzpah* for Adam to tell Hashem that not only did he sin once but he will do so again. Adam's statement, however, is not brazen *chutzpah*, but rather a cry of despair. Having sinned, it is always harder to refrain from doing so a second time. Adam was saying, "If I couldn't stop from sinning when I was perfect, how am I going to stop from doing so again?"

And that is exactly what we think to ourselves as well: "I've being losing my temper for 40 years, and pounding my chest about it on Yom Kippur for as long as I can remember, so how can I realistically hope to do any better this year? If *teshuvah* means that *HaKadosh Boruch Hu* knows that we will never do a particular sin again, how am I ever going to do *teshuvah*? I myself do not even believe that I will not sin again, so how can I expect Hashem to believe it?"

⚜ TWO TYPES OF TESHUVAH

But despair is not conducive to *teshuvah*. In fact, the despair we have been describing is itself one of the biggest impediments to *teshuvah*. To change ourselves, we first need the confidence that change is possible. A sense of futility is the Evil Inclination's strongest weapon.

To fight the despair engendered by past failures, it is helpful to remember that *teshuvah*, too, comes in stages and that there are many levels of *teshuvah*. Rabbi Akiva says in the last *Mishnah* in *Yoma* (85b), "Happy are you, Yisrael. Before Whom are you purified and Who purifies you? — Your Father Who is in Heaven." Rabbi Akiva brings two prooftexts in support of his statement: "I will sprinkle upon you purifying waters and you will be purified" (Yechezkel 36:25); "The Mikveh of Israel is Hashem" (Yirmiyahu 17:13).

This *Mishnah* is problematic. Why did Rabbi Akivah have to bring two separate verses in support of his statement? To answer this question Rabbi Hirsch Spector, the son of Rabbi Yitzchak Elchonon Spector, pointed out that there are two types of halachic purification in water. In one, the person is required to completely immerse himself in a *mikveh*; in the other, it is sufficient for the *Kohen* to sprinkle even a drop of specially prepared water upon the person for him to become ritually pure again. Similarly, said Reb Hirsch, there are two types of *teshuvah*. One is a complete *teshuvah*, which can be symbolized by total immersion in a *mikveh*. But there is another level of *teshuvah*, which can be symbolized by the sprinkling of one drop of special water. The latter type of *teshuvah* is less complete, less dramatic; it builds up over the years, drop by drop, until a complete *teshuvah* is achieved.

The *Chafetz Chaim* gives a beautiful parable to illustrate this latter type of cumulative *teshuvah*:

> *A merchant made a large order with the wholesaler with whom he usually did business. The wholesaler prepared the order and presented the merchant with a bill. At that point, the merchant pleaded with his supplier for an extension of credit because he was short of cash. The wholesaler was inclined to agree until he looked up the merchant's credit record and saw that he already owed a large amount and had been derelict in his payments over a long period of time. Being a good-*

hearted soul, the wholesaler still considered giving into the merchant's entreaties until his credit manager intervened and insisted that no further credit be extended. "This guy owes us thousands of dollars, he never pays, and his word is worthless. How can you think of giving him credit on another large order?" the credit manager asked incredulously.

With that, the merchant began wailing piteously and begging for one last extension of credit. A third merchant who happened by at that moment and overheard what was going on could not resist getting involved. He suggested that his fellow merchant order a much smaller amount and pay for it in cash. With the goods purchased, he would earn enough to come back and make another order. And in this way, he would over time be able to pay off the debt in small increments.

The credit manager balked at even this suggestion and pointed out that the man would no longer be purchasing enough to be entitled to wholesale prices. At that, the first merchant again started begging that he at least be able to continue buying at wholesale prices, and the kind-hearted wholesaler agreed. With new resolve, the merchant went about building up his business, and over the course of a few years, working steadily, if unspectacularly, he was able to pay off his whole debt.

We are that merchant, writes the *Chafetz Chaim*, Every year we come to Hashem and tell him that we want to do *teshuvah* wholesale: no more *bittul Torah*, no more lashon hara, no more anger. And He says to us, "I know you. You said the same thing last year." Nevertheless, we beg for one more chance, and the Merciful One is inclined to grant it. Then the Satan intervenes and points out our past record in alarming detail. At that point, our only chance is to tell Hashem, "O.K., no more wholesale *teshuvah*. This year all I'm asking for is the chance to improve myself a bit. Nothing flashy, but something within my grasp, something that will allow me to feel myself growing in a tangible way." That is, for us, the only possible route. And it works.

I once received a letter from a woman who heard me speak on this subject in one of the annual *teshuvah* lectures. She wrote that after hearing the address she realized that her words had become meaningless. Over and over, she would find herself saying that she was going to do something and then not keeping her word. So last spring (note that *teshuvah* is not restricted to *Erev Yom Kippur*) she undertook to keep her word in two specific areas. She resolved to be on time for all appointments, and not to promise to be someplace at a particular time if she really had no idea when she would be able to make it. And secondly, she resolved not to threaten her children with punishments that she knew she had no intention or ability to carry out. No more, "If you hit your little brother again, you don't go out for a week." These were her only two resolutions. But the results were not limited to these two areas. She wrote, "I find myself measuring my words much more carefully in other spheres as well to make sure that they are true." That is "retail *teshuvah*" — *teshuvah* in small, achievable steps.

Kayin taught this lesson to his father Adam. Kayin was doing *teshuvah* for having murdered his brother Hevel when he met his father. Adam asked him, "What was your judgment?" and Kayin told him, "I did *teshuvah*, and I was reconciled (נתפשרתי) to the *Ribbono Shel Olam*." Adam cried out in amazement, "Such is the power of *teshuvah* and I never knew it!"

What can it mean that Adam had never heard of the power of *teshuvah*, which was created before the world itself? Do *Chazal* not tell us that Adam spent 130 years in the most intense forms of *teshuvah* after his sin (*Eruvin* 18b)? Rabbi Dov Weinberger in his *sefer Shemen HaTov* offers a beautiful explanation of this *Midrash*. Adam, he writes, knew about only one type of *teshuvah* — the type of complete *teshuvah* that the *Rambam* describes in the second chapter of *Hilchos Teshuvah* where a person finds himself in exactly the same situation as that in which he sinned previously, with his desire for the sin unabated, and he does not sin. What Adam learned from Kayin was that there could be a *teshuvah* that did not meet all the *Rambam's* conditions — the *teshuvah* of sprinkled waters, not the *teshuvah* of complete immersion in the *mikveh*. The verb used by Kayin to describe his reconciliation with Hashem — נתפשרתי — is from the same root as פשרה, *compromise*. Kayin's was a *compromised teshuvah*, but *teshuvah* nevertheless. And that is the *teshuvah* that we must seize upon today, the *teshuvah* of small improvements, year after year.

❧ THE POWER OF TESHUVAH

Adam and Kayin are, of course, not the only famous *ba'alei teshuvah* (penitents) in *Tanach*. Others include Yehudah, Reuven, and David *Hamelech*. But one that is probably not that well remembered from our studies of *Tanach* is Yechaniah (also referred to, in Melachim II 23:8, as Yehoyachin), one of the last kings of Yehudah. Yet it is this Yechaniah to whom the *Rambam* (*Hilchos Teshuvah* 7:6-7) refers in his famous description of the power of *teshuvah* to transform instantaneously the relationship between man and G-d.

Yechaniah was a terrible *rasha* — so terrible that Hashem says of him, "If Yechaniah, the son of Yehoyakim, king of Yehudah, were the signet ring on My right hand [which is never removed], I would cast him aside" (Yirmiyahu 22:24). And Hashem swears that Yechaniah will die childless without an heir of his to sit on the throne of Yehudah (Yirmiyahu 22:30).

Yet it is this very Yechaniah to whom the *Rambam* alludes when he writes, "How great is the power of *teshuvah*. Last night he was completely separated from Hashem, the G-d of Israel. . . . He cries out and is not answered. . . . And today he cleaves to the Divine Presence. . . . He cries out and is answered immediately. . . ." (*Hilchos Teshuvah* 7:7).

How did this transformation in Yechaniah take place? The *Midrash* tells us that when Nevuchadnezer conquered Jerusalem, he took Yechaniah captive and threw him into a dungeon. At that point, Yechaniah had no children and the Sanhedrin realized that if he were to die in the dungeon without descendants the whole Davidic dynasty would be cut off. Therefore the Sanhedrin prevailed upon Nevuchadnezer to allow Yechaniah's wife to be lowered into the dungeon in the hope that they would produce a child. But before Yechaniah could be with his wife, she told him that she had just become halachically forbidden to him.

Yechaniah, whom Hashem Himself had described as worthless, then did something completely out of character: He refrained from touching his wife. Hashem saw his *teshuvah*, and when his wife was subsequently lowered into the dungeon again, she conceived a child named Shaltiel. Shaltiel fathered Zerubavel, who in time led the Jewish renaissance in *Eretz Yisrael*. So great was the power of Yechaniah's *teshuvah* that Hashem Himself annulled His own vow that he would die childless. And just as Hashem had once described Yechaniah as a signet ring to be cast aside, so did he later describe Zerubavel, the product of Yechaniah's *teshuvah*, as His signet ring (see *Hilchos Teshuvah* 7:6).

In one moment of *teshuvah*, Yechaniah not only changed his life and that of his descendants, he changed the course of the history of *Klal Yisrael*.

There is yet another lesson to be learned from Yechaniah besides the power of *teshuvah*. And that is how precious a moment can be, and by extension how precious is life itself. Sometimes, especially when we are younger, we tend to forget this and think of life as endless. That is what Rabbi Shimon bar Yochai had in mind when he explained Hashem's verdict on His creation as follows: "and behold it was good" — this refers to the Angel of Life; "and behold it was very good" — this refers to the Angel of Death. Without the realization that our lives come to an end, we would never appreciate how great is the gift of life. Only the awareness of the Angel of Death makes life "very good."

The *Mishnah* in *Gittin* gives us various tests to discern the development of a child's understanding. The first level is whether if he is given a nut and a stone, he will throw away the stone and retain the nut. The next stage is whether he can be lent something for a period of time and recognizes that it must be given back when that time is over. A child who can play with a friend's toy and give it back when it is time to go home has reached a new stage of maturity.

This last test, says Rabbi Avraham Pam, applies to us as well. Do we recognize that life is something that has been lent to us for a period of time, but that we will soon have to return to our Maker? If we do, we are adults. But if we do not act on this realization, then we are still children no matter how old we are.

The famous *Maggid* of Kelm once called upon his audience to imagine that all those buried in the Kelm cemetery could suddenly come back to life for a half an hour: "What would they do? This one would run to the *beis medrash* to learn, and this one to the hospital to visit the sick, and this one to help out a poor widow. All the while, each of these reprieved souls would watch the clock to see how much time was left." The

Maggid concluded his *shmuess* by asking, "*Rabbosai*, if we have more than a half an hour, is that so bad? Does every moment then cease to be precious? Is that a reason to not keep our eyes cocked on the clock all the time to make sure we are not wasting time? And who can really be sure that he has more than a half an hour?"

Those last words took on special poignance for me soon after reading this *shmuess*. I was sitting in the Ner Israel *beis medrash* at 11:30 one Thursday morning confident that I knew the course of the coming day. As usual, I would give my *shiur* in half an hour. After that, I would return home for lunch, do some Shabbos shopping, and then return to the *beis medrash* for *Minchah* and afternoon *seder*. At the end of *seder*, I would return home for supper, pay a few bills, and at 9 p.m. go to the Agudah *shul* to give my Thursday night *shiur*, as I do every week.

Just then a man came into the *beis medrash* carrying a brown paper bag and asked to see a rabbi, and someone directed him to me. As he approached, I rose to give him a *Shalom Aleichem*. I remember wondering what he had in the paper bag, when suddenly he dropped the bag, took out a knife, and began trying to stab me. He later told the police he had awakened that morning and heard voices telling him to kill a rabbi. At noon I was not giving my *shiur* as I had planned; I was sitting in an ambulance instead. (*Baruch Hashem*, I was barely scratched.)

There is a bookseller in Brooklyn who learned the same lesson in another way. Someone once asked him why he is always smiling, and he answered, "Because I'm alive." It seems that he had been in London on business and was scheduled to return to America. He asked an acquaintance which cab company to call for the airport and was told that there were two cab companies — one that never comes on time and one that is always punctual. Somehow he became confused and called the company that is always late, and sure enough the driver was late, and he missed his flight. That flight was

Pan Am flight 103 which blew up over Lockerbie, Scotland, killing everyone on board. Knowing that one was meant to be on a plane that crashed gives a new perspective on life. Since that day a smile has rarely departed from that bookseller's lips.

Sometimes we experience something that wakes us up and forces us to realize how rich life is. I was once asked to address a group of counselors at the Hebrew Academy for Special Children (HASC). I was invited to come at 9 p.m. to *daven* with the counselors before speaking, but for some reason when I got there I was directed to a room in which a group of severely retarded adults was *davening*. Frankly, I was very shaken to find myself in that room. For one thing, I doubted that we had a kosher *minyan* and, in addition, everyone seemed to be staring at me. Up until *Krias Shema* some of the group had been *davening* and some not. But at *Krias Shema* everyone suddenly started shouting at the top of their lungs. Normally, in *shul* everyone says *Shema* with the same *nusach* and *niggun*. This *Shema*, by contrast, was a discordant cacophany, literally a *geshrei*, a "primal scream *Shema*." It sent shivers down my spine.

I remember two other exceptional *Shemas*. The first was more than thirty years ago, the day my father and I arrived in Baltimore from Seattle and we *davened Ma'ariv* in the yeshiva for the first time. The second was when 20,000 Jews recited *Shema* together at the *Siyum HaShas* in Madison Square Garden. At the time, I was sure that the *Shema* at the *Siyum HaShas* was the most powerful one I would ever hear until the coming of *Mashiach*. But I want you to know that it did not compare to that *Krias Shema* with a group of severely retarded adults. I was left with a permanent reminder of what can be accomplished with a single *Krias Shema*.

A student of mine, who had previously studied at Columbia University, once returned to New York to run a Shabbaton for a group of mentally handicapped teenagers. He was speaking about each Jew's individual task in life, how each letter in the Torah represents a different Jewish *neshamah* and how each letter must be clearly separated from those around it because each Jew's task is different from that of every other Jew. At that point one of the boys raised his hand and asked: "What's my role in life? I'm retarded; I don't have a role." With that, he started crying and was joined by many of the advisors.

My student who was running the Shabbaton thought quickly and answered, "Look what you did with your question. You made a whole room of people start crying; you made people think and evaluate their lives. Even here, you have a role."

A week later that same boy awakened and told his mother that he did not feel well. Later that day, he died. My *talmid* went to be *menachem aveil* (console the grieving). He had no idea what he could say to comfort the parents, so he spoke to them of the previous week's Shabbaton. He told the parents about their son's question, and how with that question he had perhaps come close to fulfilling his task. The boy's parents were comforted.

✑ THE ULTIMATE CHALLENGE OF YOM KIPPUR

We have seen how much one mentally handicapped youngster can achieve with a single question or a group of severely retarded adults with one *Krias Shema*. And if that is the case, how much more so do we who have been blessed with normal, healthy lives have to ask ourselves: What is my purpose in life?

In the final analysis, thinking about that issue is what Yom Kippur is all about. And when we reflect deeply on this question, we will realize that there is only one answer to the question of the purpose of life: Torah and mitzvos. That answer remains the same — though it will take an infinite variety of individual forms — whether we are rabbis, homemakers, accountants, or lawyers. Whatever our profession, a Jew's life is defined only in relation to Torah and mitzvos.

The *Shelah HaKodesh* cites the Jewish custom of reciting various verses whose first and last letters correspond to our names upon the completion of *Shemoneh Esrai*. The reason, explains the *Shelah*, is so that we will not forget our names when we arrive in the Heavenly Court and are asked who we are. This explanation is not immediately understood, for it would seem a lot easier to remember our names than to remember all the verses. Rabbi Chaim Dov Keller comments therefore that the *Shelah* did not mean literally that the verses will help us remember our names; rather, the verses are designed to help us remember our identity as Jews. They are a constant reminder that the root of our souls is in the Torah and our identities cannot be separated from a mitzvah in the Torah.

Sefer Yonah, which we read at *Minchah* of Yom Kippur, teaches the same lesson. Yonah is on a boat being wracked by waves and heavy winds, and he is asked, "Yonah, what is your work?" Yonah does not answer that he is a member of the prophets' guild. Rather, he replies, "I am a Jew, and Hashem, Lord of the Heavens, do I fear." For a Jew there is no other way to identify himself.

A Jew once came to the Brisker *Rav*, and the Brisker *Rav* asked him what he did. The Jew answered by telling him what business he was in. The Brisker *Rav* asked again: "But what do you do?" This time the Jew was genuinely confused and replied by telling the Brisker *Rav* how much he earned a year. To this the Brisker *Rav* told the man, "That's what G-d does for you. But what do you do?" The only answer to that question is Yonah's: I am a Jew, and I fear Hashem.

The question we have to confront on Yom Kippur is: How close am I to saying that my identity is a verse in the Torah? How close am I to defining myself as Yonah did — as a Jew and nothing more or less. The closer we come to answering these questions affirmatively, the closer we will be to ensuring a favorable judgment for ourselves and our loved ones.

Four Questions For Yom Kippur

✎ THE ENIGMA OF KOL NIDREI

K ol Nidrei occupies a very special place in the heart of the Jewish people. Even Jews far removed from any observance, who are never seen in a synagogue of any type, will dutifully appear once a year for the *Kol Nidrei* service. There are dozens of *niggunim* (melodies) for nearly every part of the *davening*, and yet virtually all of *Klal Yisrael* uses the same *niggun* for *Kol Nidrei*.

In truth, the hold of *Kol Nidrei* on the collective imagination of the Jewish people is, at first glance, more than a little difficult to fathom. The prayer itself contains none of the dramatic power or the gripping story of courage and martyrdom that led to the composition of *U'nesaneh Tokef*. Nor does *Kol Nidrei* evoke images of the scales dangling between life and death. *Kol Nidrei* is, in fact, an extremely technical prayer, a cancellation of various forms of vows that one may have taken in the preceding year.

In attempting to account for the importance of *Kol Nidrei*, the *Levush Mordechai* explains that there are really three categories of mitzvos. We are all familiar with two categories: mitzvos between man and his fellow man, and mitzvos between man and G-d. But, says the *Levush Mordechai*, there is a third category that might be termed mitzvos between man and himself. When a person takes an oath, he in essence gives his word, and the quality of his word defines him. Thus by structuring the Yom Kippur *davening* to begin with *Kol Nidrei*, *Chazal* are hinting to us that the main theme of the day is this confrontation with ourselves in front of G-d.

Strange as it may sound, most of us do not have very much time to spend with ourselves. Our days are so busy that we rarely have time to consider our internal, spiritual state. The masters of *mussar* developed the idea of a separate room to which one could repair for inner reflection and self-scrutiny, and Chassidim used to have what they called a "dead hour," a period of time just to sit and think. Such practices, however, seem to the modern Orthodox Jew as quaint relics from quiet, simpler times.

The time for self-scrutiny grows smaller and smaller by the day, as the profusion of modern technology increasingly intrudes into every moment of the day. Years ago a person might at least use the time commuting to work for some contemplation of his soul. Today, in a society that abhors silence, people spend the commute listening to the "talk shows" or cassettes.

The idea that our task on Yom Kippur is confronting ourselves is further hinted to in the verb "to confess" in *Lashon*

Hakodesh. The positive mitzvah of Yom Kippur is *vidui*, confession of one's sins. Apart from confessing, there is no explicit mitzvah of *teshuvah* (repentance) in the Torah. Interestingly, in *Lashon HaKodesh* the verb "to confess," להתוודות, is found only in the reflexive form, like להתלבש, to dress *oneself*, or להתרחץ, to wash *oneself*. Ever so subtly, then, the word conveys the message that we must confess to ourselves, even as we confess in front of G-d.

◆ THREE CHEERS FOR GUILT

When we confess to ourselves in front of G-d, one of the likely consequences is guilt. Guilt is a frowned-upon emotion today, something we try to deny rather than deal with. Try to reprimand your children, and you are more likely than not to hear, "Hey Abba, you are trying to guilt trip me."

To be sure, there is much guilt that is both unhealthy and unwarranted, but guilt itself is crucial to our spiritual development. Guilt is to the soul what pain is to the body. Pain warns us that something is wrong and must be attended to, and guilt fills the same function with respect to our souls: It alerts us that we are not fulfilling the purposes for which we were created.

Another *mashal*: Guilt is like hunger. If we developed a pill that completely suppressed hunger, eventually we would starve to death. Similarly, guilt is the soul's warning that it is being mistreated, that something is amiss. Where guilt is suppressed or swept under the rug, there is no possibility of remedying the underlying injury to the soul.

To avoid guilt we rationalize and make excuses for ourselves. Shlomo *Hamelech* succinctly summarized the history of mankind: "G-d made man straight and they sought out all form of calculations [i.e., excuses]" (Koheles 7:29). Before the sin come the rationalizations to permit it, and afterwards all manner of excuses to avoid the guilt. At the very beginning, Hashem gave Adam only one mitzvah — do not eat from the tree — and even this was too much. And with the first sin went the first excuse, "The woman that You gave to be with me — she gave me of the tree..." (Bereishis 3:12).

Soon afterwards came the second sin: Cain killed his brother Hevel. The verse reads, "Cain said to his brother Hevel. And they were in the field and Cain rose up against his brother Hevel and killed him" (Bereishis 4:8). There is something missing here: What precisely did Cain say to Hevel? *Targum Yonasan ben Uziel* in fact supplies the missing dialogue, but the question of why the Torah omitted it still remains. Rabbi Yosef Harari-Raful gives a beautiful answer to this question. The Torah omits Cain's words because they are irrelevant. Whatever he said was nothing more than a rationalization of what he was about to do. It makes no difference what the particular excuse or rationalization was because there will always be one — whether it be one's wife, boss, kids, job, or lack of job. So the Torah tells us in effect, "What he said is immaterial" — if it would not have been this rationalization it would have been another.

⚓ TAKING RESPONSIBILITY

The natural consequence of this pattern of excuse and rationalization is the inability to take individual responsibility for our actions. *U.S. News and World Report* once ran an editorial on the "It's Not My Fault Syndrome." Criminal defenses today are limited only by the *chutzpah* and imagination of defense attorneys. When an "addiction" to Hostess Twinkies is a defense for homicide, we have reached the end of personal responsibility. This attitude that nothing is ever my fault — I was compelled by forces beyond control — is an absolute bar to *teshuvah*. If I cannot control my actions, why should I repent for them?

Rabbi Chaim Friedlander, the late Ponevezh *Mashgiach*, showed how overcoming this attitude is the message of the famous story of Elazar ben Dordaya in *Avodah Zarah* (17a). Elazar ben Dordaya was so notoriously hedonistic that he had visited every possible harlot. Then he heard of one across the sea who charged a fortune for her services. Elazar ben Dordaya undertook the long journey and paid her a fabulous sum. Before he sinned with her, she remarked on his obsessive immorality, saying that he was so gross that it would be impossible for him ever to repent.

Her words pierced him to the very depths of his being. Suddenly he lost all interest in her services. All he sought was to return to Hashem. Elazar ben Dordaya felt incapable of doing *teshuvah* on his own and sought help from the sun and the moon, from the stars and the constellations, from the heavens and the earth, and from the mountains and hills. Each in turn told him that they were incapable of helping him. The intermediaries from whom Elazar ben Dordaya sought assistance can each be understood as another form of rationalization that human beings use for their behavior. The stars and constellations, because they are permanent and unchanging, represent one's natural endowments, and their refusal to help him is thus a denial that our behavior is determined by our inherited traits. The mountains (הרים) represent one's parents (הורים), and their refusal to help is a denial that our behavior is determined by how our parents raised us. The heavens and earth represent the remaining environmental forces, and their refusal to help is a denial that environment is destiny.

Finally, Elazar ben Dordaya had to confront the fact that his life depended on him alone. No one else was responsible for the mess he had made of it, and no one else could begin the repair. At that moment, he sat down, placed his head between his knees and began sobbing until his soul departed. With his passing, a *bas kol* (Heavenly voice) went out, "Rabbi Elazar ben Dordaya has been accepted for eternal life." When the great *Rabbeinu HaKodesh* heard of this incident, he cried and said, "Some attain the World to Come in a lifetime, and some in a moment." In that one moment of complete repentance, Elazar ben Dordaya even merited the title rabbi, teacher, for from him we learn both the power of *teshuvah* to atone and that the beginning of *teshuvah* is the acceptance of one's own responsibility, the recognition that we, and no one else, have distanced ourselves from G-d.

Lest anyone think that such a dramatic *teshuvah* experience could only occur in the times of the *Gemara*, Rabbi Berel Wein tells a story of a completely assimilated Jew who was surprised by the heavy traffic out of Manhattan one night and rolled down his window to ask a policeman what was going on. The Irish cop's answer, "Don't you know tonight is Yom Kippur?" was like a sharp slap across the face. The man was shocked to find how far he had strayed from the Jewish people and eventually became a *ba'al teshuvah*.

We all know the story of David *Hamelech* and Batsheva. Though the *Gemara* concludes that David was not guilty of any sin, the prophet Noson came to him and challenged him to explain, "Why have you despised the word of Hashem and done this evil in His eyes? Uriah Hachiti [Batsheva's husband] you killed with the sword, and his wife you took for yourself as a wife..." (II Shmuel 12:9). After the prophet finishes telling David all the terrible things that will befall him as a consequence of his sin, there is a break in the verses. Before David begins his response, there is a very unusual empty space in the text.

The Vilna Gaon explains that this unusual spacing represents a moment of hesitation on David's part. On the one hand, he knew that technically he had been justified in sending Uriah on a suicide mission, and that upon Uriah's death, Batsheva would have become retroactively divorced even before David laid eyes on her. On the other hand, he also knew that the prophet's curses came not from him but from Hashem. So David hesitated, but in the end he admitted, "I have sinned against G-d." And Noson responded, "Hashem will remove your sin and you will not die." Because David admitted that he had sinned, his *teshuvah* was accepted.

Though in many respects David's sin was greater than Shaul's when he failed to kill Agag, the Amalekite, David retained his kingdom and Shaul lost his. Shaul did not respond in the same way as David, but rather blamed the people for his misplaced show of mercy, and by failing to accept responsibility showed himself unworthy of kingship.

✎ A LOOK INTO THE MIRROR

Yom Kippur forces us to look into the mirror and examine ourselves. When we do so, we must be careful to look close up and not from too great a distance. From a distance, we might think to ourselves, "Not too bad. Compared to the rest of American Jewry, we are fine Jews indeed." If so, we would do well to contemplate an insight of the Brisker Rav on *maftir Yonah*, which we read at *Minchah* on Yom Kippur. The Brisker Rav's message was that it is those of us who know of Hashem's presence in the world upon whom the fate of the Jewish people depends and who are responsible for the tragedies that befall us.

Yonah found himself on a storm-tossed ship surrounded by idol worshipers. It would have been the easiest thing in the world for Yonah to convince himself that Hashem's anger was directed at the idolaters and not him. Yet Yonah knew better: "On account of me is this great storm upon you" (Yonah 1:12), he told the sailors.

And it is the same today. Ninety percent of the Jews in the world were raised without any knowledge of Hashem at all. They are not accountable; it is not they who are preventing

Mashiach from coming; we are. So make sure that the look in the mirror is a close one.

≈ FOUR QUESTIONS WHILE LOOKING IN THE MIRROR

We all know the Four Questions asked at the *Seder*. I would like to suggest four more questions — only these questions are for Yom Kippur and they are addressed to ourselves and not our fathers.

The first question is: How is my mitzvah observance? "Oh, that's an easy one," you might say. "I keep *kashrus*, Shabbos, and *taharas hamishpachah*." Let me quote, however, from a speech given at a communal dinner by a Mr. Hillel Gross, who davens in a *shul* with a large number of *ba'alei teshuvah*:

> *I think it's important that you ba'alei teshuva, B.T.'s, have some how idea of how we F.F.B.'s [frum from birth] feel about you. Frankly, we don't like you very much, and I'd like you to to know why.*
>
> *For ten years you've been coming to my house for Shabbos and Yom Tov, and we've talked about your past and how you became religious. Now for once I'd like you to try to see things from my perspective. I am what sociologists would call a "tired Jewish business-man." My ideal Friday night is to daven as fast as I can, eat as fast as I can, jump under the covers, and sleep comfortably until Shacharis.*
>
> *... Then after we wash, we sit down, and inevitably during the course of the conversation, usually mine, one of you will interrupt with the greatness sincerity and ask, "Excuse me, isn't what you're saying lashon hara?"*
>
> *"Well, yes, I suppose you could say it's lashon hara," I*

respond lamely. Fine, no more lashon hara. Then you want to sing, and you are especially partial to the zemiros that have eight verses…

I exaggerated. We do not really dislike you; it's just that you make us uncomfortable. We're uncomfortable because after twenty, thirty, forty years of saying Shemoneh Esrai three times a day, the sight of you davening with such vitality and exuberance forces us to consider whether perhaps our Shemoneh Esrai has become flat, routine, mechanical.

We are uncomfortable because we ask ourselves in the depths of our souls — and do not think for a moment that we don't — whether we could have done what you have done at twenty or thirty or forty. Could we have uprooted the habits of a lifetime, changed occupations, confused our friends, and antagonized our families out of a commitment to Judaism?

And if we articulate this question, know that few of us dare answer it.

So that is the first question: Has your performance of mitzvos become flat, mechanical, stale after years of repetition?

The second question is: What really makes me happy? What gives me joy in life?

The question is not just whether we have joy in the mitzvos, but whether they constitute the chief joys of our lives. There is a frightening *Arizal* on this point. In the course of our history, unfortunately, all the curses in the Admonition [*Tochachah*] of *parashah Ki Savo* have been fulfilled. In the midst of enumerating all the calamities that will befall us, the Torah attributes them to one cause: "…because you did not serve Hashem, your G-d, with joy and goodness of heart, amidst plenty" (Devarim 28:48). The charge, writes the *Arizal*, is not that we had no joy in mitzvos, but that our joy in mitzvos was not greater than our joy in our affluence. Nowadays, too, we live in an affluent society, and we, too, will be judged not just by whether we keep the mitzvos, not even by whether we delight in them, but by whether our joy in mitzvos exceeds our enjoyment of our luxurious houses, fancy cars, and vacations.

Let me just give two examples of what it means to live for mitzvos. The two conversations I am about to relate may not seem like anything earth shattering, but they capture an attitude towards life to which we should all be aiming. The first was with a young man who had learned in *kollel* for many years and is now in sales. In the course of a conversation, he mentioned to me that he had made a sale that day which would bring him a nice bonus for the month. But, he added wistfully, "It's still not like coming home after a full day in the *beis medrash*."

The other example is a simple Jew who was kind enough to drive me from a lecture in Boro Park to Penn Station. To tell you the truth, I was not too taken with him initially, especially when his first question was: "Why do they have to bring someone from Baltimore to lecture in New York?" I had him pegged for the typical New Yorker who thinks the world ends at the Verrazano Bridge. But in the course of our conversation, this Jew started talking to me about the importance of *davening* in his life. It turns out that he has not missed a *minyan* in 17 years. Not once in that time has he failed to recite *Krias Shema* before the earlier *Magen Avraham* deadline or *davened Maariv* prior to nightfall. He used to vacation every year in Florida but quit because it was too difficult to find *minyanim* en route. Every Shabbos morning, he recites the entire *sefer Tehillim* prior to *davening*.

I do not know if this Jew can even learn *Mishnayos*, but I do know that after talking to him for a half an hour, I emerged from his car a humbled man. I knew I had been in the presence of a person who is assured a place in the World to Come.

The *Rambam* in his commentary on *Mishnayos* writes that *Hakadosh Baruch Hu* gave us so many mitzvos in order that every Jews can find a particular mitzvah to which he clings with special care. And if he does that, he surely has a place in the World to Come. That being true, it is clear that a Jew whose joy in life lies not in his possessions but in the fact that he has not missed a *minyan* in 17 years has a bright place awaiting him in the World to Come.

What we value will effect us not just in this world but in the World to Come. There is an old saying that a person should be careful about what he prays for because he just might get it. So it is with us. *HaKadosh Baruch Hu* pays us off in our own currency.

The *Chiddushei HaRim*, founder of the Gerrer dynasty, was once walking along the road when a wagon driver passed by and offered him a ride. After a few miles, one of the horses suddenly dropped dead. A few miles further, the other horse followed suit. The wagon driver had lost his whole source of livelihood in a matter of hours, and he got out of his wagon and sobbed piteously until he too died on the spot. Not too long after that the *Chiddushei HaRim* had a dream, and he saw the wagon driver in Heaven as a reward for his kindness to the *Chiddushei HaRim*. And what was his reward? A beautiful wagon drawn by two magnificent steeds.

We make our own *Olam Haba*. If your goal in life is to be a named partner in your law firm, with your name on the door, that may be your *Olam Haba*. And if a BMW is the object of all your desires, you may get that too. But think how you are going to feel when all you are given is a permanent seat on the 50-yard line or a beautifully decorated home — and a simple Jew you never paid attention to in *shul* is basking in the light of the *Shechinah*.

When I was a little boy, I spent the better part of one summer trying to fashion a slingshot for myself. All my whittling never came to much, but once I saw a big plastic slingshot in a store window and asked my parents to buy it for me — something they wisely refused to do. Just think how embarrassed I would have been if at my *bar* mitzvah my parents had presented me with "just what you always wanted" and it had turned out to be a slingshot. How disappointed I would have been that my parents did not realize that I had outgrown slingshots. Let us not be left with our own various forms of slingshots in the World to Come.

The third question for Yom Kippur is that asked of Yonah by the captain of the ship: "What is with you, sleeping one?" (Yonah 1:6). Cataclysmic events are taking place before our eyes, and we remain in a slumber. The world we have known for a lifetime is turned topsy-turvy; and we are brain dead to even ask whether there could be a message here for us, much less what the message might be. In the space of a few years, we watched one of the two great superpowers, the Evil Empire, implode and self-destruct before our eyes. In the course of its self-destruction, there were coups and countercoups, and for days it was not even known who had his finger on the world's largest nuclear arsenal.

With the disappearance of the Soviet Union, hundreds of thousands of Jews are suddenly free to leave. Do we realize what that means? Near the end of the *Chafetz Chaim's* life someone ran to tell him a rumor that Stalin was dead. The *Chafetz Chaim* did not even lift his head. He had only one question: Are children learning Torah in Russia? Today the answer is that many people *are* learning Torah in the former Soviet Union, and some — albeit too few — of the grandchildren of the Russian Jewish children of the *Chafetz Chaim's* day are learning in *Eretz Yisrael* and America as well.

The same year the Soviet Union unraveled, a madman aimed his missiles, potentially armed with poison gas or agents of biological warfare, at *Eretz Yisrael*, and we witnessed miraculous salvation from those missiles. No doubt that grabbed our attention for a while, but when the show was over did we think seriously about its implications or internalize any lessons from it?

And today, there is a government in Israel willing to give away huge chunks of the Land for will-o'-the-wisp promises of peace, promises for which there is neither support in the Arab street nor among the elites. Jewish blood is suddenly cheap in a state that boasted that it had overcome Jewish weakness once and for all. Hundreds of thousands of Jews are being placed in imminent danger, and where it will stop short of the Mediterranean no one can foresee. Is all of this even disturbing our sleep? Or does it remain business as usual?

In our own communities, we hear of terrible tragedies one after another, and unless the victim is someone close to us, we cluck our tongues, perhaps even say a few chapters of *Tehillim*, and consider that we have done our duty. Rabbi Itzchak Isaac Sher once addressed a group of retired rabbis before Rosh Hashanah, and he told them that they should not be too complacent about a favorable judgment.

> *Gentlemen, you are all fine Jews, and you do not sin. Yet you pick up The New York Times in the morning, read that a man was killed, and you drink your coffee. How can you drink coffee when you read that a woman became a widow and children lost their father? You should faint in anguish, but you do not. You do not care enough how that death affects other people.*[1]

Can we fail to realize that the Attribute of Strict Judgment is ascendant over the Attribute of Mercy? In response to similar tragedies, the *Chafetz Chaim* wrote in *Ahavas Chesed* that we as a people have the means to reverse strict Heavenly judgment by showing the same kindness to others that we beg *Hakodesh Baruch Hu* to show to us.

Charity (*tzedakah*) and kindness (*chesed*) are our only

---

1. Bunim, *A Fire in His Soul*, pp.. 63-4.

hope of altering Hashem's manner of relating to the world; they are the cosmic button influencing the judgment above. When we show our concern with the downtrodden and suffering among us, we necessarily effect the judgment above. In his last years, Rabbi Ruderman once asked a certain yeshivah student to *daven* for him. The *bochur* thought the Rosh Yeshiva was just trying to make him feel good — after all, what could his prayers add to those of the Rosh Yeshiva — and laughed. With that, the Rosh Yeshiva became upset. That boy went every Friday to visit a senile, old man in a nursing home, and the Rosh Yeshiva felt that the prayers of one who was doing such an act of kindness would have a special power to arouse Divine mercy. His irritation was at the young man's failure to recognize the power of his own capacity for kindness.

The fourth question is: Am I really yearning for *Mashiach*?[2]

I am not going to predict that *Mashiach* will come this year, or next year, or even the year after that. But he will come. The signs are there, and we would all do well to consider what that means for us.

Nearly fifty years ago, a Jew in Toronto asked Rabbi Yaakov Kamenetsky whether *Mashiach* would come that year, and in his typical fashion Reb Yaakov returned the question, "What difference does it make to you?" The Jew told Reb Yaakov that he kept his store open on Shabbos, but that if *Mashiach* was coming he would close his store. That Jew desecrated the Shabbos in public, but he knew it made a difference that *Mashiach* was coming.[3]

The measure of our desire for *Mashiach*, as we have dis-

---

2. For a full treatment of this issue see Chapter 16 "Are We Really Yearning for Mashiach?"

3. Reb Yaakov's answer also bears remembering. He told the Jew that Mashiach was not coming immediately. His wife asked him in amazement how he could have said such a thing, especially in light of the fact the Jew was willing to close his store on Shabbos. Reb Yaakov told her that the *Rambam* rules that a Jew who does not believe in the coming of *Mashiach* has no portion in the World to Come. On the other hand, nowhere does it say that a Jew who desecrates Shabbos has no portion in the World to Come. Since this man obviously had retained his belief in *Mashiach*, Reb Yaakov was unwilling to do anything to endanger that belief. He wanted the man to ignore anyone who promised him that *Mashiach* was coming soon in order to preserve that faith.

cussed elsewhere at length, is our efforts to extirpate baseless hatred from our midst, since it is that hatred that delays the Redemption. The *Sefer Mitzvos Gedolos* mentions another aspect of preparing for *Mashiach* that is relevant to us. He writes that we have to be extremely careful to avoid anything that smacks of deceit or stealing, no less with gentiles than with Jews, because when *Mashiach* comes and the *Ribbono Shel Olam* brings us back to *Eretz Yisrael*, the nations of the world are going to be watching with awe. If we steal and cheat, then they are going to shake their heads and wonder how Hashem could have chosen such a people, and that will be the ultimate desecration of G-d's Name. But if we are honest, then they will nod and acknowledge how right Hashem was to choose such honest, polite, considerate people, and our Redemption will truly bring the knowledge of Hashem to all the world.

⬥ THE BEST DAY OF THE YEAR

When I was younger I used to be puzzled by the statement in the *Gemara* (*Taanis*) that *Klal Yisrael* had no better days than Yom Kippur, which seems to assume that Yom Kippur is the happiest day of the year. As I've grown older, however, I have found that assumption to be true: Yom Kippur is the highlight of the year, the one day when I feel I've shed my earthly shackles. It is no longer a day that I cannot eat, but a day that I do not need to eat. It is a day completely free from all material concerns: No need to worry about one's clothes while wearing a *kittel*. No telephones; no distractions of any kind. A day to just sit in *shul* wrapped in your *tallis* and soar. A day of cleansing; a day to get in touch with one's spiritual root.

Above all, it is a day to feel Hashem's closeness and how much He desires that we return to Him. Do you think it was only a harlot who told Rabbi Elazar ben Dordaya that he could no longer do *teshuvah*? Do you think it was a traffic cop who responded to a completely assimilated Jew, "Don't you know it's Yom Kippur?" That was G-d speaking. We are told that everyday a *bas kol* (Heavenly voice) goes out from Sinai bewailing the loss to mankind caused by their distance from the Torah. And do you know where the holy books locate that Heavenly voice? Within ourselves. The only problem is that we have so deadened our souls that we do not hear it.

Yom Kippur, however, is the day for peeling away the layers of encrustation from our soul and hearing that *bas kol*. "You give Your hand to sinners and Your right hand is extended to receive penitents," we say in *Ne'ilah*, the closing prayer of Yom Kippur, and the *Zohar* comments that Hashem sticks out His hand as if to a man foundering in the dark.

Vacations help even though we return to the same problems we left behind, and Yom Kippur is a vacation for the soul, a day when it escapes the limitations of our physical bodies. Even though we return at nightfall to our daily concerns, we are not the same. By freeing our souls for that one day and sensing our nearness to our Loving Father, Who is patiently awaiting us, we are better able to change. We can reach out for the hand that is extended towards us.

Yom Kippur day calls out to us, "Do something different, for G-d's sake and yours, grab His hand."

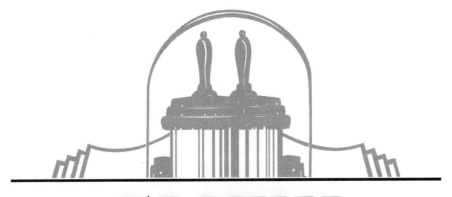

FAMILY

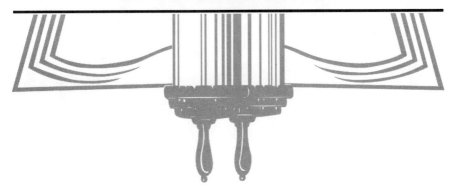

The Toughest Job You'll Ever Have: Raising Children

T here is no task to which we devote more time and energy than the raising of our children. The *Haggadah* interprets the word עמלינו, *our toil*, to refer to our children. One of the major commentators explains that children are referred to as "our toil" because the main goal to which all our striving and efforts are directed is the production of fine children.

Our own and others' evaluations of our success or failure in life depends largely on whether we succeed in raising G-d-fearing, fulfilled, successful children. Each of us knows people who for all outward appearances have been successful in virtually all their endeavors, and yet who view their lives as failures because they did not produce the type of children for which they hoped.

The first commandment given to mankind was פרו ורבו, which is usually translated as "be fruitful and multiply." Rabbi Samson Raphael Hirsch, however, offers an alternative interpretation. The word רבו, he says, is not derived from רב, *numerous*, but from רבוה, *to shoot* or *aim*. The Torah is telling us that our task as parents is not just to have children, but to guide them to the goal for which they were created.

◆꙰ "TRICKLE DOWN" PARENTING

The process by which we guide our children is usually referred to as *chinuch habanim*, the education of children. But that, says Rabbi Yaakov Kamenetsky, is a misnomer, for parents are not primarily *mechanchim*, educators. Rather they are *mashpi'im*, ones who influence. The root of the word משפיע, said Reb Yaakov, is related to שפוע, *something inclined*. Parents are like a slanted roof in relation to their children. Everything they do, everything they say, flows down from them onto their children and leaves its effect, though often not the one we intend. That is what I like to refer to as Reb Yaakov's "trickle down" theory of parenting.

Educators — *rebbeim* in yeshivas, Bais Yaakov teachers — attempt to transmit information, as well as ways of assimilating that information, to our children in a direct fashion. The influence of parents is, by contrast, indirect. But while indirect, it is also pervasive. The *Zohar* (*Parshas Va'eschanan*) has a homiletical interpretation of familiar phrases in the *Shema*:

"Teach them thoroughly to your children and speak to them while you sit in your home. . . ." When do we teach our children? asks the *Zohar*. And it answers: When we are sitting in our homes.

The way our actions affect our children was once brought home powerfully to me. It was one of those hot, muggy Baltimore days when all you can think about is getting back inside an air-conditioned room, and I was trudging along on my way to the yeshiva when I realized that I had forgotten to *bentsch* (recite *Bircas Hamazon*). The last thing in the world I wanted to do was to *schlep* back home again, and I stood there trying to think of any possible reason for not doing so.

First, I tried to convince myself that I had *bentsched*. When that failed, I considered continuing on to the yeshiva and *bentsching* there. Unfortunately for me, there are many *poskim* who hold that one must *bentsch* in the place he ate and even *bedi'avad* (after the fact) one has not fulfilled his obligation if he *bentsches* in another place. I was stuck.

I went home and sat down to *bentsch*. Meanwhile, my daughter came into the kitchen and was surprised to find me there since she knew I had already left for the yeshiva. She asked me what brought me home, and I told her that I had forgotten to *bentsch*.

"You came back to *bentsch*?" she asked me. At that moment, I knew I had scored. After years of reminding her to *bentsch* from a *siddur*, to *bentsch* aloud, that *bentsching* is a mitzvah *d'oraisa*, in this one inadvertent act I had achieved more than with all my lectures.

But if parental example can be the most effective way of inculcating our values, it can also be the greatest impediment to our children's acceptance of the message we are attempting to convey. Let's say your son comes home with a note from his teacher that he lied in school. You give him a lecture full of every statement of *Chazal* you can think of on lying: תתן

חותמו של הקב"ה אמת ,אמת ליעקב, *Give truth to Yaakov;* HaKadosh Boruch Hu's seal is truth.

Ten minutes later, the phone rings. You're lying down on the couch, and your son comes over and tells you that there's a phone call. You're exhausted and you tell him, "Say I'm not at home." Out the window went your entire lecture. You lost him because he saw that you don't tell the truth either — no matter what you preach.

Similarly, the words that our children hear coming out of our mouths when we are not trying to teach them anything are likely to leave at least as big an impression as those that are directed at them. The verse in the Book of *Mishlei* (27:21) reads, "The refining pot is for silver, and the furnace for gold. And a man is tested by his praise (איש לפי מהללו)." Rashi and the Targum understand this last phrase to mean that we can judge a person by his reputation, by the praises, or lack of them, that others say about him.

But Rabbeinu Yonah understands the phrase differently: A man is judged by that which he praises. In *Pachad Yitzchak,* Rabbi Yitzchak Hutner gives an example of what Rabbeinu Yonah meant. A businessman who learns only two hours a night, writes Rabbi Hutner, can actually be at a much higher spiritual level than a *kollel* member. How so? If the *kollel* member spends his time at home talking about this person's successes in business and someone else's killing on the stock market, he shows himself to be a businessman at heart. Money is what he praises. The message he conveys to his children is that money is what counts, and that's the message his children will pick up.

On the other hand, a layman whose greatest pleasure is to honor a Torah scholar, who makes it clear that the highlight of his day is the hour or two he spends learning at night, lets his children known that learning is the most important thing in life.

What we say to our children, the values we emphasize, trickle down like water off a slanted roof.

EDUCATE THE YOUTH ACCORDING TO HIS WAY

The staple of all those who write on child-raising is Shlomo *Hamelech's* advice: "Educate the child according to his way" (Mishlei 22:6). What is often left out is the end of the verse: "for when he grows up he will not depart from it." What is the "it" from which he will not depart? Rabbi Shlomo Breuer, the son-in-law and successor to Rabbi Samson Raphael Hirsch, interpreted the verse to mean: Educate the child according to his own way *because* when he grows up he will not depart from *his way*. In other words, a child has a certain innate nature — his own particular temperament and personality, his special talents and weaknesses. Those are with him for life. Our job is to work with those traits, not against them, because they are not going to change.

I was once at a meeting of the education committee of a certain yeshiva, and there was an intermission during the meeting. I started flipping through some old yearbooks that I found lying around. Next to each picture, the students had written their goals and aspirations. It was fascinating because I knew many of the people in the pictures. What was so interesting was how little my friends had changed from what they were 20 years ago. What they were at 18, they are at 38.

I have a friend who loves numbers. One of his biggest thrills is calculating the time of the *molad* (New Moon). Now, anyone who has ever learned this subject knows it is an extremely complex subject. Whenever I find myself in a *sugya* having to do with the *molad*, my brain seems to shut off. But my friend is just the opposite. He tells me that he recently ran into his kindergarten teacher and she told him, "You know, when you were a little boy, all the other children used to play with balls and fire engines. But you sat on the side of the room with the blocks that had the numbers on them, and you used to play all day with those blocks."

The *Gaon* makes the same point about natural inclinations in his commentary to *Mishlei*. There he quotes the *Gemara* in *Shabbos* (קנו) that one who is born under a certain sign of the Zodiac will become a spiller of blood. Rabbi Elazar says he might be a *mohel* or a murderer, a doctor or a highwayman — but one way or another he's going to be a spiller of blood.

"If you take a child and try to make him act contrary to his nature," says the *Gaon*, "he may listen to you when he is young out of fear, but as he grows older, he will throw off your yoke from his neck and turn from [the direction you have pointed him]." Therefore the job of parenting is not imposing our desires on our children, but asking ourselves, "What do I have here?" and then working with that. We should not throw up our hands in futility, but, on the other hand, we should not try to make our children into something they are not.

A father may dream that his son is going to be an all-star basketball player. The father pushes his son to practice dribbling and shooting, but unfortunately the boy only grows to be 5'5" and is no athlete. All that is left in the end is a frustrated father and a bitter child.

If these phenomena were confined to Little League or basketball, it would be one thing, but they are part of our world too. We have also seen the damage when a father decides his son is a future *rosh yeshiva*, if not the next *gadol hador*. Often these aspirations have no relation to reality, and the result is a child who feels like a failure because he has disappointed his father.

That's what Shlomo *Hamelech* is telling us. Discover your child; learn who he is, not who you would like him to be. And then work with his talents and personality to raise a well-adjusted, secure child.

Now let us turn to an area that causes all of us difficulty as parents: how to criticize or punish our children when they have done something wrong. This encompasses everything from getting them to brush their teeth or do their homework to correcting a superficial learning of the *Gemara*.

Again we turn to the wisest of all men, Shlomo *Hamelech*: "Do not rebuke the scoffer lest he hate you; rebuke the wise man that he will love you" (Mishlei 9:8). On the surface, this verse would seem to refer to two completely different people: one a scoffer and one a wise man. The *Sheloh Hakadosh*, however, explains that the verse is talking about two aspects of each of us — the fool and the wise man within.

The message of the verse then becomes: Address the wise man in the one you seek to criticize, not the fool within him. Call him a fool, or treat him as such, and that is how he will behave. On the other hand, treat him like a person of understanding, and he will become one.

When you criticize your child, don't tell him, "You *should* know better." Tell him, "You *know* better." The difference is subtle but crucial. The second way addresses him as a person of discernment and wisdom. The child who is spoken to in that fashion will not experience your criticism as a blow to his self-esteem and walk away feeling worthless.

When your child does something wrong, do not label *him* or *her*; label the *act*. If your child tells you a lie, don't call him a liar. When you do that you define his essence as one who lies. Instead, label the act: "That's a lie." The difference is immense. The opprobrium of the act is not diminished, but the child is left with the sense that he is still good.

The verse in which we are commanded to give reproof to our fellow Jew concludes ולא תשא עליו חטא, which is usually translated, "And do not bear responsibility for his sin." But Rabbi Gedaliah Schorr once said that the words לא תשא could also be understood in the sense of "Do not raise." In other words, do not raise or magnify the sin. Give reproof without blowing up the sin. Focus instead on the sinner and lift him up. Tell him that he is too elevated to behave in such a fashion.

Rabbi Abraham Twerski, the well-known psychiatrist from Pittsburgh, often speaks of the way his own father offered criticism. He used to say *"Es past dihr nisht —* That way of acting is not befitting for you; it's beneath you." By telling his children that they were above such behavior, he lifted them up.

Avi Shulman writes in his book *Candlelight* that criticism is like pepper; it should be used sparingly. Like pepper, criticism is very useful. A little bit in just the right amount, at the right time, is one of the parent's most powerful weapons. But just as the overuse of pepper only results in dulling the taste buds to the point that it loses all its effectiveness, so does too much criticism result in children who grow deaf to whatever you are trying to convey to them.

Children have to learn how to deal with criticism. We make a big mistake if we try to shield our children from it entirely. Without criticism, children have no means of knowing what is expected of them, what is right and what is wrong. Criticism helps them establish the boundaries of what is acceptable and what is not. Moreover, criticism is inevitable; no one is immune.

But the way our children respond to criticism — whether it be from a boss, a *rebbi,* or a spouse — will have a lot to do with how they experience it growing up. If criticism was used as a punishment, a way of withholding love, then when the child grows up, he will react to criticism, from whatever source, with anger.

Every Jewish parent knows the verse חושך שבטו שונא בנו, which is commonly translated as, "Spare the rod and spoil the child," but more literally means, "One who spares the rod hates the child." From this verse, we might think that the Torah advocates corporal punishment — a good smack every once in a while. But that is not necessarily the case. If if were, then the verse should end, "And one who loves him will multiply his blows." But that is not so. Rather the verse ends, "And one who loves him offers him *mussar*." The child should know that there is a rod hanging on the wall, but the Torah tells us that there are plenty of other ways to punish the child rather than with the rod.

The verse in Zechariah (11:7) reads: "I took two rods, and one I called Pleasantness and one I called Destruction." How can a rod be called Pleasantness? Rabbi Shlomo Wolbe explains that positive reinforcement is a perfect example of "pleasantness," and when someone withholds a compliment, that, too, can be considered a rod. So can a sharp look or an expression of disappointment. There are plenty of rods other than hitting, and Shlomo *Hamelech* is talking about these and not physical abuse.

A child requires discipline, he needs and wants to know that there are limits. But hitting is rarely the most effective way of bringing home that message. That is not to say that there are no occasions when a slap is appropriate for a younger child. But even then there is one crucial condition: One should never strike a child out of anger.

Do not take out your frustrations on your children. We live in an extremely tense world. A father may come home from the office all wound up; he's had it with his boss, he's had it with his associates. Then his child makes the mistake of choosing that day to do something wrong and he ends up on the receiving end of what his father would really like to give to his boss. Such a slap has no place. A slap is only appropriate if it is administered in a calm fashion to a child who is not too old to be hit.

Shlomo *Hamelech* also teaches us that "the wounds of one who loves are effective" (Mishlei 27:6). But the wounds must be administered by one who loves and is perceived as such. Even when you punish your child, he must always realize that this is punishment meted out by one who loves him and seeks his well-being, not one who, G-d forbid, hates him.

To illustrate this point, I would like to share a story told to me by Rabbi Moshe Eisemann about one of the leading German rabbis at the turn of the century. His name was Rabbi Shlomo Carlebach, and he had six sons, many of whom became famous rabbis in Germany in their own right. He insisted that his sons come to *minyan* on time every day. If they failed to come on time, the punishment was immediate: They did not receive jam on their bread at breakfast. But whenever one of the sons was denied his jam, Rabbi Carlebach would not take any jam either. Those children never doubted their father's love even as he punished them; they had concrete proof of how much it hurt him to deny them something.

◄ THE LOVE BOND

As parents, we must never lose sight of the fact that the bond of love is the primary tool we have going for us. Destroy that bond and everything is lost; preserve it, and you will never lose your child. Rabbi Wolbe warns that if we scream enough, and hit enough, and punish enough, there will come a time when that bond of love is broken. For a parent there is no greater tragedy.

Someone recently recommended a biography of a boy growing up in a strict Mennonite home. This family was extremely poor; they had nothing beyond the bare necessities. The boy had nothing of his own besides the clothes he wore and his shoes. The home was austere, and the son viewed his father as a cold and distant figure. The father was a hardworking farmer, who used to supplement his income by slaughtering his pigs from time to time. One day the boy did a job for a nearby farmer, and the man gave him a pig as a present. That pig became his most prized possession. He raised the pig and won a prize for it at the county fair.

A few years after the boy received the pig, the family had a very difficult summer — the harvest was terrible, the apple crop was spoiled. They literally had nothing to eat. The father had no choice but to slaughter his son's pet pig, and the boy experienced a flash of hatred for his father.

The man put his hand on the boy's cheek and tried to comfort him. Then he did something the boy had never see him do before. He cried. And the boy, who had just lost his most precious possession, fell upon his father and started kissing him over and over again to show him his love.

Where there's love, you can even take away a child's prized animal and it does not matter. But if you destroy your child's natural love, you will pay the price. That is something that we should never forget when we are punishing children.

I do not want to sound like a "Spock" parent. We see all around us the results of child-raising without limits, without discipline. But at the same time, we must never lose sight of the fact that there is, in Rabbi Wolbe's words, "no greater destroyer of the love between parents and children than a parent who creates an atmosphere of excessive fear in the house."

Twenty-five years ago, I doubt that I would have had to tell parents that they must spend time with their children. But unfortunately, that must be emphasized today in our generation of working mothers and working fathers. This does not mean that mothers should not work outside the home. Some of the best mothers I know work. But what it does mean is that both parents must make a special effort to spend time with their children.

To try to ease the burden of guilt on parents who do not have enough time for their children, the term "quality time" has been coined. If you have "quality time" with your child, we are told, then it does not matter how little time you actually have for them. But to quote one New York City principal, "Without quantity time, there is no quality time." If you do not spend time with your children you send them a message loud and clear: You do not rate very high on my list of priorities.

Another principal wrote recently, "Spend time with your children or your child will force you to spend time with him — whether in the principal's office, the courtroom, or the hospital." Children will find a way of getting that time out of you, but if they have to wring it from you, it will not be quality time, it will be terrible time.

I once heard of an *adam gadol* whose children did not turn out as well as he had hoped. As he was bemoaning his failures as a parent, he mentioned a simple layman whose children were each better than the next. And he asked aloud, "What was the difference between him and me?" He answered his own question: "When I was sitting learning *Rambam,* he was singing *zemiros* with his children."

Speaking of *zemiros* raises another crucial point. We are very good, by and large, in educating our children in mitzvos — the do's and don'ts. But at the same time, we must remember to instill the enthusiasm for mitzvos, the feeling of delight in doing mitzvos. Children should not experience mitzvos as a burden, but as the most enjoyable aspect of life.

Rabbi Dessler writes in a letter that the goal of every educator (which includes parents as well) must be not only to transmit information, but to convey the holiness and love of mitzvos. As a matter of pedagogy, for instance, there are no doubt better ways to teach reading than those employed in *chadarim*. But the method we follow has proven itself over the generations as ideally suited to exciting a child with the letters of the *aleph-bais*.

If we want our children to feel excitement in doing mitzvos, we have to show it ourselves. We have to burn the *chametz* with them, put up the *succah* with them. I once heard my *Rosh Yeshiva*, HaRav Yitzchak Yaakov Ruderman *zt"l*, ask someone if he had put up his *succah* yet, and the man replied that he had hired someone to do it. When the *Rosh Yeshiva* pressed him as to why he had not done it himself, the man replied that he was all thumbs.

Rav Ruderman told him, "I remember my father putting up the *succah*. He would put it up and it would fall down. Then he put it up again, and it would fall down again." As he said this, however, I could see that what was left with the *Rosh Yeshiva* was not the effort of putting up the *succah* again and again. What remained all those years later was the memory of his father's excitement in building the *succah*.

That excitement is the primary thing we have to give over. There is a time to observe every detailed requirement mentioned in *Mishnah Berurah*, but first our children have to experience the enjoyment, the fun.

I was once speaking in Detroit and an older European man came up to me afterwards and said, "Tell *bnei Torah* to sing with their children. It used to be that the singing was the centerpiece of the Shabbos table." Now it seems that the more religious we want to appear, the bigger the scholars we view ourselves as, the less we sing. And this is a terrible mistake.

In general, there is much we could do to return the Shabbos table to what it once was. There used to be an expression in Yiddish (actually it still is in Yiddish, it's just fallen into disuse), "*Nisht fahr de kinder* — It's not for the kids." Today the Shabbos table is too frequently the place for discussing *shul* or yeshiva politics. If I want my children to quiet down at the Shabbos table, all I have to do is start talking politics with our guests. Then they'll stop and listen attentively.

We pay a heavy price, however, for sharing these issues with our children. They become prematurely sophisticated and lose the natural *temimus* (innocence) of youth. There is plenty of time for them to learn about *shul* politics, but the Shabbos table is certainly not the place.

❧ RESPECT FOR TEACHERS

As parents, we are partners with our children's educators (*mechanchim*). That being the case, it is crucial that we not act in such a way that will lessen their respect for their teachers. Not only does showing *rebbeim* and teachers a lack of respect make it harder for them to educate our children, it will eventually come back to haunt us in a lack of respect for all authority, including ourselves. We have to build up the *rebbeim* and teachers in our children's eyes. When we, for instance, refer to them by their last names — "Is that what Rosenberg said?" — we do just the opposite.

At the same time, it is crucial for teachers and *rebbeim* to be careful not to diminish their students' respect for their parents in any way. Just to give some idea of how important it is never to destroy a child's respect for his parents, consider this advice that the *Chazon Ish* once gave to teachers of children whose parents were Shabbos violators. The *Chazon Ish* warned them to be very careful never to do anything to lower the parents in their children's esteem. Without respect for parents, he told them, all education is impossible.

When Reb Yaakov Kamenetsky was a *rav* in Toronto, the *minyan* in his *shul davened* on Shabbos past the proper time for saying *Shema*. A group of educators told Reb Yaakov that they wanted to make another *minyan* that would *daven* at the proper time. But Reb Yaakov, with his unbelievable insight and wisdom, told them not to. If you do that, he told the educators, you are giving the children the message that their parents are not so religious, that they are not doing something right. And it is not worth the price to put down parents in the eyes of their children. (Reb Yaakov himself *davened* alone at the proper time, and then went to *shul*. In *shul*, he reviewed the *mishnayos*, to make it appear as if he was *davening*, so as not to insult his congregants.)

❧ THE FINAL INGREDIENT

Even parents who follow all the rules that we have discussed — appreciating your child for who he is, being sparing and constructive in criticism, punishing with love, not out of anger, spending time with the children — cannot succeed as parents without one final ingredient: *siyata deShmaya* (the help of G-d, Heaven). Without it, all our efforts are in vain.

And if we want Hashem's help, we have to remember to ask for it. When we *daven* in *Shemoneh Esrai* for understanding and knowledge and wisdom, let us remember to specifically ask for these things in our child-raising.

Tanna D'vei Eliyahu tells us that a person should seek Divine mercy for himself, his children, and all the members of his house that they not come to ways that are ugly in Hashem's eyes. I heard once from Rabbi Yaakov Kamenetsky that when he first came to America he was very hesitant to bring his children here, for in those days America was one great wasteland compared to Lithuania, from where he was coming.

What did he do? He prayed that his children would all remain observant (*shomrei* mitzvos). He did not ask anything more from the *Ribbono shel Olam* than that. And at the end of his life, he often expressed his gratitude to the *Ribbono shel Olam* that all his children and grandchildren had remained religious.

Tanna D'vei Eliyahu relates the story of a *Kohen* who is described as "fearing G-d secretly." This *Kohen* had six sons and four daughters. And everyday he would prostrate himself and lick the dust with his tongue and pray that none of his children should ever sin. In other words, he prayed for success with his children. And the *Midrash* continues, "Before the year was over, Ezra came and *HaKadosh Boruch Hu* took the Jews, including the *Kohen,* from Babylonia." That *Kohen* did not die, *Tanna d'vei Eliyahu* relates, until he had seen his children serve as *Kohanim Gedolim* and young *Kohanim.*

Shalom Bayis: Can This Marriage Be Improved?

N o matter how good our marriages, there is always room for improvement in *shalom bayis* (marital harmony). Once Rabbi Aryeh Levine, who was immortalized in the book *A Tzaddik In Our Time,* noticed that some of those who *davened* in a little *shul* near his home in Jerusalem did not treat their wives properly, and he asked permission to speak after *Kabbolas Shabbos* one week. His words were intended for one Jew in particular.

Needless to say the man to whom Reb Aryeh had been directing his remarks did not show any indication that he recognized himself in Reb Aryeh's words. But after the *davening* none other than HaRav Isser Zalman Meltzer, one of the greatest *roshei yeshiva* of the previous generation, thanked Reb Aryeh profusely for his words and assured him that they would help strengthen his own *shalom bayis*. To fully appreciate Reb Aryeh's surprise you must know that Reb Isser Zalman was renowned for the perfection of his character traits. When he was still a young man, one of the leading *roshei yeshiva* in *Eretz Yisrael* today went to visit Reb Isser Zalman. After that meeting, he found himself crying from *chalishas hada'as,* an overwhelming feeling of inferiority in the presence of one greater than oneself. What caused him to cry was not Reb Isser Zalman's genius in Talmud but the beauty of his *middos,* a beauty so profound the young man could never imagine attaining it.

In any event, Reb Isser Zalman assured Reb Aryeh that he had moved him deeply and made him aware of his own failings in this area. In that pre-computer age, Reb Isser Zalman wrote out his monumental *Even HaAzel,* one of the most important modern commentaries on the *Rambam,* by hand. But since his handwriting was very poor, his wife used to copy it over for the printer. Occasionally she made mistakes in copying, and the sight of errors in his *divrei Torah* occasionally led Reb Isser Zalman to express irritation. It was for sensitizing him to his failings in this area of *shalom bayis* that Reb Isser Zalman thanked Reb Aryeh Levine.

If we consider the nature of marriage, it is no surprise that there is always room for improvement in *shalom bayis*, even for the greatest of *tzaddikim. Hakodesh Baruch Hu* is described as He Who makes peace in the Heavens. To what does this refer? To the fact that the angel of fire and the angel of water can coexist right next to one another in the Heavens despite their opposite natures. How is this possible? Because Hashem gives them one common desire: to fulfill His will.

Similarly, *shalom bayis* is not the harmony of two identical people, but the harmony of two people with different personalities, different backgrounds, different desires — two people who may be like fire and water to one another. Somehow these two distinct people have to learn to live together, to solve their problems together, to become, ideally, like limbs of the same body. And they have to do this in the pressure cooker of the home, where there are problems of money, problems with the children, and where they are far removed from the public eye, which so often serves as a restraint on our worst behavior.

❧ THE IMPORTANCE OF SHALOM BAYIS

It would be almost impossible to overstate the importance of *shalom bayis*. The *Gemara* in *Chullin* (141) notes that the Divine Name itself was erased in the process of testing the Sotah Woman, even though it is otherwise forbidden to ever erase the Divine Name. That erasure of the Divine Name was permitted, however, in this case in order to bring about peace between a man and his wife. *Avudraham*, the famous commentator on *tefillah* (prayer), explains that women are freed from all mitzvos that must be done at a particular time because of the importance of *shalom bayis*. Were a woman not freed from these obligations she would find herself frequently torn between her household duties and the performance of the mitzvah, and that might lead to arguments in the house. The prevention of such arguments, then, is a sufficient reason to free women from taking a *lulav*, hearing the *shofar*, and reciting *Krias Shema*.

When after many years of being barren Rachel *Imeinu* finally gave birth to a son, she called him Yosef, because G-d had removed (אסף) her shame. Her shame would seem to refer to the humiliation of being a childless woman, but *Rashi* cites a striking *Midrash,* which states that God's blessing to her was so all-encompassing that it embraced even seemingly trivial areas of life, such as casual household annoyances. Once a woman has a child, the *Midrash* says, if her husband inquires about a broken dish, she can tell him his son did it, and because of his great love for his son he will be mollified. Similarly, if he comes home and finds all the figs eaten, she can once again place the blame on her son.

This *Midrash* is, to say the least, a little puzzling. Are we meant to believe that until Yosef was born, Yaakov *Avinu* used to come in from a hard day in the fields and complain about broken dishes or a missing snack? Or that after Yosef was born, Rachel *Imeinu* used to defend herself by saying, "Oh, our little darling Yossi has been at it again." Certainly, our Patriarch and Matriarch did not argue about leftovers and broken dishes.

The *Midrash* teaches the importance of *shalom bayis* by stressing its importance in the eyes of the *Avos.* Rachel knew that even the slightest possible friction between husband and wife, the slightest feeling of irritation upon finding the house not just so, is a potential hazard to *shalom bayis.* And therefore she expressed her joy that even this threat was removed with Yosef's birth.

✒ THE CONSTANT CHALLENGE

I am neither a marriage counselor nor a practicing rabbi, but I do teach young men of marriageable age, and many of them come back to talk to me after they are married. In almost every case, there is some feeling of disillusionment. Most of us who have been married a few more years can still remember the shock of our first argument with our new spouse. That first argument hits these newlyweds particularly hard — in part because they have been raised on the concept of romantic love in which everyone lives happily ever after. And if there is more than one fight, and they do not seem to be getting along, it does not take long for them to start worrying that they made a huge mistake and that theirs was not a good match.

There is no way to fully prepare young *chassanim* and *kallos* for an experience that is essentially different from anything they have previously experienced. First, they did not really know each other. Before marriage, who thinks to ask, "How do you squeeze the toothpaste?" But differences in squeezing the toothpaste are only a trivial example of the larger quandary. Now for the first time, they have to learn to live in the greatest intimacy with another person, who may be to them like fire to water.

Nor does the problem disappear just because we are fortunate enough to survive our first year of marriage. Life is full of changes. People change over the years. You have children, they grow up, and before you know it they leave the house. You acquire new interests, make new friends, drop old ones. As one psychiatrist put it, "Spouses have to be like astronauts — always making mid-course corrections." Unless we learn to make those accommodations and mid-course corrections, the potential for conflict in any marriage can overwhelm us.

The *mezuzah* on the doorway to our homes can serve as a good metaphor for successful marriage. According to *Rashi*, the *mezuzah* should be vertically on the door, while according to *Tosafos* it should be placed horizontally. To resolve this difference, we do something that is almost never done in halachah: we split the difference between these two positions, and place the *mezuzah* at a slant. The *mezuzah* is the first thing that one sees on entering the home, and it should convey an important message for all of us: You cannot be rigid if you want a secure, happy home; you have to learn to bend and compromise.

Shalom Bayis: Can This Marriage Be Improved? ☐ 87

As a little boy, I learned about divorce for the first time. Later, after my parents had some little argument or another, I remember asking my mother, "Are you going to get divorced?" My mother smiled and shared with me what was for her one of the eternal verities: Jews do not get divorced. Later that became: Religious Jews do not get divorced. But today even that is not true. Religious Jews do get divorced — and the numbers are soaring. And if the number of divorces is climbing, we can assume that this is only the tip of the iceberg as far as serious *shalom bayis* problems are concerned.

What has changed so much since I was a boy? Why has what was formerly taboo even for non-religious Jews become commonplace even among the religious? The loss of taboo itself is one of the causes of the ever escalating divorce rates. People simply do not enter marriage with the same assumptions they once did. When one begins a marriage with the assumption that this is forever, it has serious implications for the way one approaches every other aspect of marriage. If you have to remain with this spouse forever, you have a tremendous incentive to work on your marriage and to learn how to live happily together. On the other hand, if marriage is only for so long as its immediate advantages outweigh the disadvantages, why invest much energy in making it work?

Some lawyers today routinely advise all couples before marriage to make pre-nuptial agreements explicitly detailing who gets what in the event of divorce. What message does it convey to couples if plans are already being made for the divorce before they have even gotten to the *chuppah*?

We live today in a throwaway society where nothing is forever. It is not just aluminum cans and foil that gets thrown away after one use. Try taking in a clock radio for which you paid fifty dollars last month for a repair. The fellow in the repair shop will barely glance at it before grunting, "It doesn't pay to fix it." (Learning how to grunt that sentence is apparently the major thing that is taught in repair school today.)

"What do you mean it doesn't pay to fix it?" you ask in amazement. "I bought it last week." But the repairman just gives you one of those looks that suggest you have been living on another planet for a decade. And this attitude that it does not pay to fix things spills over into every aspect of our lives. First, it is clock radios that aren't worth fixing, but soon it is marriages too. And where there is no inclination to work together, to try to fix things, there is no chance of a fulfilling, happy marriage.

Finally, for perhaps the first time in human history, selfishness is no longer viewed as a vice. Our society not only fosters self-centeredness and the pursuit of our immediate gratification, it tells us there is nothing to be ashamed of. As the columnist George Will put it, we live in a generation that believed the Michelob commercial — "You can have it all" — and had its heart broken. Our democratic, legalistic society emphasizes rights but not duties; everything today is viewed as an entitlement. As one writer in *The New York Times Magazine*, the Weekly Reader of the yuppie generation, said recently, "It is a generation which was brought up thinking of exciting jobs, wonderful houses, great marriages, and beautiful children as things that come naturally — as something we deserve just by virtue of being alive."

People with such heightened expectations of what is coming to them are likely to lack the primary ingredient of a successful marriage: the capacity to give. As Rabbi Eliyahu Dessler tells us, giving causes love to grow. Giving is not the outgrowth of love, as we so commonly think, it is the *cause* of love, and where there is no giving there can be no love. "The strong bond of love between man and wife," writes Rabbi Dessler, "can only be achieved when both accustom themselves to giving to one another. Then their love will never cease and their lives will be filled with happiness."

We love our children so much because we give so much of ourselves to them: we get up in the night with them, we diaper them, we help them with their homework, we share their joys and setbacks, we worry about them, we sacrifice so that we can give them more. But the capacity to give is stifled in a society that encourages selfishness. We live in an age of 2.2 children per family (and even lower among the better educated) because big families are viewed as too much of a bother. To have a large family, you have to give to others, and people just do not want to make those sacrifices today.

❧ HONOR HER MORE THAN YOUR OWN SELF

The *Rambam* in *Hilchos Ishus* gives this definition of a husband's obligations to his wife: A man is commanded to honor his wife more than himself and to love her as himself. The respect of which the *Rambam* speaks includes how a husband treats his wife in private and in public, and it includes everything from the most sublime forms of honor to the most mundane and commonplace. The major piece of advice Rabbi Aryeh Levine gave his grandson on the eve of his wedding was: "Don't leave your clothes on the floor." That too is a form of honoring your wife.

I am in contact with many young men at the time they become engaged, and it is amazing the amount of time they spend thinking about everything they want to say to say to their *kallos*. They can spend literally hours seeking advice on precisely how to express something. HaRav Avraham Pam, the *Rosh Yeshiva* of Torah Vodaath, once remarked that if people spent even one-tenth the time thinking about what they are going to say to their spouses after marriage that they do when they are engaged, a lot of marital stress would be removed.

Why does that care end at the *chuppah*? Partly because a contemporary novelist has convinced much of society that "Love means never having to say you're sorry." But nothing could be further from the Torah viewpoint. Love means always being prepared to say you're sorry. And even more importantly, it means thinking about what you say beforehand so that you will not have to say you're sorry.

So far we have discussed the husband's obligation to honor his wife more than himself and to love her as himself. But what about a woman's obligations to her husband? The *Rambam* writes that a woman should honor her husband "*yoser midai*" — literally, too much — and that he should be in her eyes like a king. There is an interesting letter from a father to a daughter on the eve of her marriage that is often used in teaching *kallos* in *Eretz Yisrael*. In it the father notes that of his contemporaries in yeshiva the single most important determinant in their eventual success — more than youthful promise, more than natural abilities — was the quality of their marriages. Those whose wives made them kings in their own homes were successful and those whose wives did not do so struggled.

Where the husband was not made to feel like a king, he dissipated energies that could have been spent in Torah in futile attempts to establish his authority in the home, and he ended up with a miserable marriage in which he was a tyrant and his wife the ever rebellious troops. On the other hand, in those marriages where the wife made her husband into a king, he was the most benevolent of rulers and she herself was honored as a queen. That is the ideal Jewish home: one in which a king and queen rule.

Part of the mutual respect that is so crucial to a happy marriage is for the spouses to respect each other's areas of expertise. Usually there are areas in which the husband considers himself more expert — e.g., *halachah*, car maintenance — and areas in which the wife considers herself more expert — e.g., child-rearing, home decoration. In these areas it's important for the other spouse not to undercut the house "expert."

But what do we do when our spouse's actions are so far from royal deportment that it is impossible to treat him or her like a king or queen? The first rule here is to remember that people, whether it be spouses or children, generally rise to the level of expectations. Someone who is treated with great respect — perhaps even more than is merited — will seek to make him or herself worthy of that respect. And someone who is treated as a *shmatte* will behave accordingly.

When we married, we obviously felt that our spouse had many positive qualities, and we were not mistaken. What attracted us in the first place is likely still there. It's just that along the way we've discovered a few less appealing traits as well. The key here is to accentuate the positive. By focusing on the positive we both increase our own love and make ourselves more easily beloved in the eyes of our spouse. *Chazal* tell us that we should dance in front of the *kallah,* praising her beauty. And that is true even if she is lame or blind. Don't look at her blemish, they are telling us, but at those things that make her beautiful in the eyes of her husband. Focus on the positive; don't dwell on the deficiencies.

❧ SHARE YOUR LIFE

Before the *chasanah* we write up *tena'im*. Many people are not too familiar with the contents of the *tena'im* since the signing of the *tena'im* generally coincides with the smorgasbord. But there is one phrase in this document which we would do well to consider: "They should control their property equally and not hide anything one from the other." In other words, they are to share their lives with one another.

From the very outset of the marriage, Rabbi Shlomo Wolbe writes in his *Kuntras L'Chasanim,* the husband should have the intention of uniting with his wife in a complete union. As "the right hand to the left hand" is the *Chazon Ish's* way of describing that union.

Our lives are so hectic today. Between work, car pools, schools, and public activities it is possible for a husband and wife to go days at a time without ever having time to talk. By the end of the day, all they can think about is finding a pillow to drop onto. But if they go too many days without sharing their aspirations, hopes, and fears, they may wake up one day and find that they are like two ships passing in the night. Little by little, they have grown apart without even realizing it, and have little in common anymore.

To avoid this, the *Chazon Ish* advises couples to learn to find those few moments every day for talking to one another. When a husband leaves the house in the morning, writes the *Chazon Ish,* he should tell his wife where he is going, and when he returns home he should share with her what happened. And, the *Chazon Ish* continues, this is true of small matters as well as large.

Two people marry to share their lives. But to share your lives, it is first necessary to share your days. Share your days, and you will share your lives.

Recently I read a case study of a twenty-two-year-old young man who was contemplating divorce. As he told the marriage counselor, his wife had nothing to talk about besides "dirty diaper stuff," and he wasn't interested in that. Someone should have told him that if dirty diapers are part of his wife's day, they should be part of his as well. Anything that is important to your spouse is ipso facto important to you. Those couples that have solid, fulfilling marriages are those in which each spouse values and shows interest in what the other is doing.

Of course, it is possible to take this sharing too far to the point where it is stifling and each partner feels that they have no independence at all. But in our fast-moving, pressured lives, the chances of this happening are almost nil.

When Rabbi Elazar ben Azaryah was offered the position of *Nasi* of the *Sanhedrin,* his response was that he would have to consult with his wife first before making up his mind. He made his wife one with him, and shared with her the most important decisions in his life. He recognized that the most important decisions of his life were necessarily the most important decisions of their life together.

❧ KEEP THE MARRIAGE FRESH

One of the great pitfalls of marriage is monotony. *Chazal* tell us that the laws of family purity were given to protect us from this monotony — "in order that a wife should be as beloved to her husband as the day they entered under the *chuppah.*" The Torah, then, has given us one way of preserving the freshness in our marriages, but that does not absolve us from the responsibility of injecting a sense of newness into our marriages. Rabbi Wolbe writes that a husband must put his mind to finding ways to create a sense of perpetual renewal in the marriage: going out for dinner, taking walks together, going on vacations.

When the angels came to inform Avraham that Sarah would have a son the next year, they asked Avraham where Sarah was. Surely the angels knew where Sarah was so why did they ask? The *Gemara* in *Bava Metzia* (87a) says that they did so in order to remind Avraham of Sarah's modesty and thereby make her more beloved in her husband's eyes.

Since Avraham was already ninety-nine years old at the time, we might ask: Did he really need to be reminded of his wife's great virtues? Was it still necessary to arouse his love of his wife Sarah? The answer is: yes. No matter how old we are, no matter how many years we have been married, we need to work on preserving the sense of freshness in marriage so that our spouses are as beloved to us as when we were first married.

⋘ SOME SPECIAL DANGERS FOR THE ORTHODOX

Over the years I have spoken to a number of Orthodox marriage counselors, and they are almost unanimous in noting that there are some aspects of our lives as observant Jews that place unique strains on our *shalom bayis*. One of these is that one or both of the spouses is often so busy with communal affairs that they do not have sufficient time for their children and spouse. Rabbi Chaim Vital, the greatest student of the *Arizal,* writes that the judgment for mistreating a spouse will outweigh any mitzvos a person does on behalf of others. One who gives loans, consoles the grieving, visits the sick, and rejoices with the *chassan* and *kallah* will have a lot of credit at the Heavenly Judgment. But if he was angry and strict in his own house or neglected his wife, that will outweigh all the good deeds done for others. One who has time for everyone besides his own spouse should not look forward to the Final Judgment.

Another danger in our homes is taking on *chumros* (stringencies) for which we are not ready. These can, at times, cause major strains, and it is worth keeping in mind that there is no *chumrah* in the world that is worth the slightest diminution in our *shalom bayis*. To be careful even about minority opinions that are not *paskened* in *halachah* is fine as long as both the husband and wife are in agreement. But *shalom bayis* is *m'kar hadin* (a basic law), and we never sacrifice what is *m'ikar hadin* for stringencies.

In this regard, it is worth recalling a story involving the *Chafetz Chaim* and his rebbi, Rabbi Nochum Horodner. To give you some idea of the level of Reb Nochum Horodner, it is sufficient to know that the *Chafetz Chaim* went to him to study his level of righteousness. The *Chafetz Chaim* was once in Reb Nochum's house during Chanukah, and it came time to light the Chanukah candles. But Reb Nochum made not even the slightest move towards lighting the candles. The *Chafetz Chaim* was too embarrassed to ask his *rebbi* why he wasn't lighting, but as the hours passed he became increasingly perplexed. The *halachah* states that the candles should be lit before everyone has left the marketplace in order to ensure the proper *pirsumei nisah* (publicizing the miracle), and that time had long come and gone. Finally, around 10:30 p.m. Reb Nochum's wife returned home, and Reb Nochum immediately rose to light the candles.

Reb Nochum knew that the *Chafetz Chaim* must have been perplexed by his behavior, and later he explained to him what had occurred: "My wife particularly enjoys being here when I light the Chanukah *licht,* and I felt that the increase in *shalom bayis* of waiting for her outweighed even the performance of the mitzvah in the prescribed fashion." (Note that this case did not even involve a *chumrah,* but the failure to perform a mitzvah as it is supposed to be performed in the first place.) Then Reb Nochum brought a "proof" from the *Gemara* for what he had done. The *Gemara* states that if one has only enough money for Chanukah lights or Shabbos lights, then Shabbos lights take precedence because the Shabbos lights bring *shalom bayis.* From this we see, Reb Nochum reasoned, that *shalom bayis* takes precedence over Chanukah candles.

◆ CREATING AN ENVIRONMENT FOR SHALOM BAYIS

Usually when we speak of *shalom bayis* we refer to the marital harmony between husband and wife. But that harmony cannot be separated from the general tension level in the home. A home in which there is a great deal of shouting between siblings and between parents and children is not one that is conducive to *shalom bayis.* Problems between husband and wife will inevitably be reflected in the tension level in the home and that tension level in turn will affect the quality of the marriage.

The *Rambam* in *Hilchos Ishus* advises the husband to be careful not to impose a reign of terror in his home and to speak to his family members gently. Even when reproving family members about the performance of a mitzvah, the *Mabit* adds, one's speech should always be gentle. Admittedly this is not always the easiest level in the world to achieve. You walk into the house after a long, hard day and immediately trip over your kid's boots in the hall. That was the 'good' kid. Preceding you down the hall, on the floor you just paid the cleaning lady to clean, are the tracks of the one who forgot to take off his boots. Finally you reach the kitchen and are cheered by the thought of your beloved eating a post-school snack. How do you know? Because the orange juice on the table is dripping onto your floor and the refrigerator door is still open. Now remember the *Rambam's* words as you approach your pride and joy's room: Maintain that gentle tone.

Why shouldn't you yell in that situation? Because as the decibel level rises in your house so will the tension level, and in that atmosphere you are far less likely than ever to obtain the response you are seeking.

So far I have been talking only about the minor irritants. As the children grow, the conflicts become more fundamental and more draining. Nevertheless you must still keep the lines of communication open, and that you can do only if you find a pleasant mode of speech with your children.

At the end of *Megillas Esther,* Mordechai's achievements are enumerated: He was viceroy, beloved by almost all his people, and "he spoke peacefully to all his offspring." This last praise means, says the *Ibn Ezra,* that he was able to speak easily to his children and grandchildren alike. Most likely, not every one of his children and grandchildren followed exactly the path he laid out for them, but he could still have a peaceful conversation with all of them, and the *Megillah* views that as his culminating praise.

In almost every aspect of educating our children we share responsibility with other educators. But there is one area in which we have almost exclusive responsibility: preparation for marriage. No matter how many lectures our children hear before marriage on their responsibilities as Jewish husbands and wives, none will have any effect compared to the example that they see in their parents' home. If they see their parents treating one another as king and queen, then the chances are good that they will treat their own spouses in the same way. And the opposite is also true: If they grow up in a home in which husband and wife are always yelling and criticizing one another, that is most likely the model they will follow since it is the only one they have. This means that the quality of *shalom bayis* that we establish in our homes is not just for ourselves but for our descendants for generations.

You have probably all heard the story of the hapless Jew who sold his priceless *tefillin,* which had been passed down in his wife's family for years, for a beautiful *esrog* — only to have his wife, in her anger at his disregard for her heirloom, knock the *pitom* off the *esrog,* rendering it unfit for use. As he examined his now worthless *esrog,* he exclaimed, "I've lost my precious *tefillin* and my beautiful *esrog.* At least let me not lose my *shalom bayis.*" He did not complain to his wife or let the incident disturb their relationship.

None of us are likely to reach that level any time soon, but let us keep those words always in mind. Nothing so accentuates the joys of life or makes the sorrows bearable as having a partner for life with whom to share them. Let us at least have *shalom bayis.*

The Hardest Mitzvah
Of Them All:
Honoring Our Parents

CRUCIAL BUT DIFFICULT

We live in a generation that throws around superlatives — e.g., best, genius — so carelessly that most have been drained of all meaning. Nevertheless, it is no overstatement to say that the mitzvah of *kibud av v'eim* (honoring one's parents) is not only one of the most central mitzvos of the Torah but one of the most difficult to fulfill.

Every morning we begin our *davening* with the *Mishnah* in *Peah* (1:1) that lists the honoring of parents among those mitzvos for which a person "eats the fruits in this world and the principal remains intact for him in the World to Come." And in *Tanna D'vei Eliyahu,* we find, "All the world belongs to *Hakadosh Boruch Hu,* and all that He seeks is that a person should honor his father and mother." These are just two examples of the many *Gemaras* and *Midrashim* that emphasize the importance of honoring one's parents.

The importance of this mitzvah is matched by the difficulty of fulfilling it properly. Rabbi Shimon bar Yochai (*Midrash Tanchuma* to *Parshas Eikev)* felt that no other mitzvah in the Torah is so hard to do perfectly. Rabbi Yochanan, whose father died while his mother was pregnant with him and whose mother died in childbirth, goes so far as to say that happy is the person who never laid eyes on his parents, for he is free of the obligation to honor his parents (*Kiddushin* 31b). Rav Zeira was also an orphan. The *Yerushalmi* in *Peah* relates that he was once bemoaning the fact that he had no opportunity to perform the mitzvah of honoring his parents, but when he learned of the stringency of the mitzvah and severity of judgment awaiting those who fail in its fulfillment, he exclaimed, "Thank G-d that I do not have a father and mother." With respect to no other mitzvah in the Torah can we imagine an *Amora* expressing gratitude for being free of the obligation of performing it.

As long as our parents are alive, we are still children. Rabbi Abraham Twerski tells a story of being approached after a speech in Montreal by a gentleman in his mid-80's. This elderly gentleman had a rather surprising request: He wanted Rabbi Twerski to visit his father in a nursing home. Rabbi Twerski was so taken aback that he agreed, and the next day found himself talking to the 114-year-old father. The father's first question to Rabbi Twerski was, "*Hoste gezen mein boychik* — Have you seen my little boy?" So even if we are still fortunate enough to have our parents at 85, at least as far as they are concerned we remain children. And as we shall see, the demands of the mitzvah only grow as our parents age, so we might as well learn how to do it right.

❧ PHILOSOPHICAL UNDERPINNINGS

The *Rishonim* and *Achronim* emphasize two basic themes in discussing the mitzvah of honoring parents. The first is that this mitzvah is one that our intellects alone would dictate. The *Gemara*, in fact, always seems to bring examples from non-Jews of exemplary *kibud av v'eim.* The famous *Gemara* in *Kiddushin* cites Dama ben Nesina as the exemplar of this mitzvah. What did he do? The Sages came to him to purchase a valuable stone needed to replace one that had been lost from the *ephod* worn by the High Priest. Unfortunately, they arrived at a time when Dama ben Nesina's father was sleeping and under his head was the key to the box in which the stone was kept. Despite all the Sages' entreaties and their offer of unimaginable wealth in return for the precious stone, Dama refused to wake his father. And in a famous *Yalkut,* Rabban Shimon ben Gamliel says about himself that despite having served his father all his life he had not reached one-hundredth of the level of *kibud av v'eim* achieved by Esav, the Evil One.

The choice of gentiles, and even the wicked Esav, as exemplars of *kibud av v'eim* is not coincidental. Rather, *Chazal* were thereby showing us that honoring parents is a mitzvah that can be derived intellectually, an obligation felt even by a gentile without the benefit of Divine Revelation. It is, says the *Maharal,* the paradigmatic *mishpat,* a mitzvah whose general outlines, if not its every detail, human beings can derive on their own.

With respect to Dama ben Nesina, *Chazal* bring out this aspect of the mitzvah in another interesting way. If you were

The Hardest Mitzvah of All: Honoring Our Parents □ 101

feeling sorry for Dosa for having lost a fortune just because his father was sleeping at the wrong time, don't. The next year a *parah adumah* (red cow) was born in his flocks, for which he was paid a sum even larger than that he had lost, since the ashes of the extremely rare red cow are necessary for purification from all *tumah* (impurity) caused by contact with the dead. The laws of the red cow are described by the Torah as the classic *chok* (law whose reason is beyond human comprehension) — "This is the decree (חקת) of the Torah . . . and they shall take a red cow, without blemish" (Bamidbar 19:2). Thus, writes the *Maharal*, for his care with respect to the quintessential *mishpat*, Dama ben Nesina was rewarded through the classic *chok*.

What is the principle underlying the mitzvah of honoring parents that causes even a gentile to be aware of the obligation? *Sefer Hachinuch* identifies it as *hakaras hatov*, the recognition of the good that others have done for us. *Hakaras hatov* entails not only an intellectual recognition of the good that we have received but also a sense of obligation to repay that good.

There can be no gratitude greater than that which we owe our parents since the gift they have given us is absolutely without parallel: life itself. Our parents have done for us the ultimate kindness — they have brought us into the world; and for that they are deserving of all the respect that we can possibly show them. And that is only part of it. As we grow up and become parents ourselves, we can better appreciate how much effort and sacrifice went into raising us, how many sleepless nights, how much time spent worrying about us. All the love that was showered on us demands reciprocity; it creates an obligation to return that love and show our gratitude.

Our feelings of gratitude to our parents are the means by which we come to experience similar feelings, at an even greater level of intensity, toward Hashem. Rabbeinu Bachye writes that by training ourselves to honor and respect our physical parents, we learn to show gratitude to Hashem, our Father in Heaven. And to the extent that we fail in this regard with respect to our parents, so will we inevitably find ourselves lacking in our relationship to Him. To precisely the degree that we lack the the quality of *hakaras hatov* will we be lacking in our service of Hashem, for the recognition of His beneficence to us personally is the foundation upon which our entire relationship to Him is built. As *Chazal* tell us, "Anyone who denies or fails to recognize the good others do for him will deny the good that *Hakadosh Baruch Hu* does for him" (*Chayei Adam Klal* 67). This failing goes right back to the first sin when Adam HaRishon showed his lack of gratitude by trying to place the blame on "the woman that You gave me."

There is a second philosophical basis for the mitzvah of honoring parents: the concept of *mesorah*, transmission from one generation to the other. The central event in Jewish history was the experience of the entire nation — over two million men, women, and children — of the Divine Revelation at Sinai. We know of that event because those who were there then told their children, who in turn told theirs, and so on throughout the generations.

The relationship between parents and children, then, is the crucial link in the chain of this transmission of tradition. Without it, there can be no transmission. The *mesorah* is built on the trust of children for their parents and their respect for their parents as those who transmit the tradition to them.

We tend to think that there is a mitzvah of *kibud av v'eim* because we have parents, and the Torah therefore teaches us how to relate to them. But that is putting the cart before the horse. The *Zohar* teaches that "*Hakadosh Baruch Hu* looked into the Torah and created the world." The world conforms to the Torah and not vice versa. The mitzvah of honoring parents does not exist because we have parents. Rather, because there is a mitzvah of honoring parents and a mitzvah of "you shall teach them to your child," *Hakadosh Baruch Hu* created a world in which we all have parents and are not spontaneously generated.

Not only do human beings have parents. The relationship between parent and child is qualitatively different from that of any other species. Human beings are born uniquely helpless and dependent upon their parents for survival, and they remain in need of constant parental nurturing longer than any other species. Furthermore, humans maintain lifelong familial bonds.

That intense and ongoing relationship is essential to the *mesorah*. The child trusts his parents because he knows that his parent loves him more than anything in the world. How does he know? Because he was so helpless, and his parents gave and gave and gave.

Obedience and reverence for parents is necessary if children are to receive the tradition intact. *Kibud av v'eim* is part of the Decalogue, explains Rabbi Samson Raphael Hirsch, because without it there can be no transmission from one generation to the next of "I am the Lord, Your G-d ..." or "You shall have no other gods before Me..."

Rabbi Meir Simchah of Dvinsk, the *Ohr Somayach*, points out that the *Gemara* has to find a proof from the Torah that a child may not listen to his parents if they tell him to violate Shabbos or some other commandment. From the fact that the *Gemara* could even entertain such a theoretical possibility, says the *Ohr Somayach*, we learn how precious is reverence for parents to the overall structure of a Torah life and to what extent it must be fostered.

The two philosophical bases governing our obligations to our parents — gratitude and tradition — explain why there are two separate mitzvos relating to parents: one of honoring our parents and one of fearing them. Honoring them, the *Gemara* says, includes feeding them and giving them to drink — i.e., taking care of their physical needs. The mitzvah to fear them requires that we stand up when our parents enter the room, that we never contradict them explicitly, that we not sit in their chairs, etc. The first set of obligations derives from our *hakaras hatov*. Because they gave us life and nurtured us, so must we attend to their physical needs. The second set of obligations is designed to engender respect for them as those who have transmitted the tradition to us. To accept the *mesorah*, I must first be in awe of the one who is its bearer.

⊷ WHY IS IT SO HARD?

An understanding of the philosophical underpinnings of the mitzvah also helps us understand why this particular mitzvah is so hard to fulfill properly. It is difficult, in part, because *hakaras hatov* itself is so difficult. We simply do not like to feel obligated to anyone else because that makes us feel dependent, and no one wants to admit that he cannot do everything himself. This instinctive denial of the good others have done for us is only intensified with respect to those whose good to us continues every single day and is felt in every breath we take.

One-time favors we can deal with — they do not threaten our independence in the same way.

My wife still talks today about a favor that a Jamaican fellow we had never seen before and will likely never see again did for us. It was July 4, 1976, and my wife and I came up with the bright idea of joining the multitudes heading for Washington, D.C. to see the Bicentennial celebration. We borrowed a friend's jalopy, and headed off for the capital. We never did make it to the fireworks that night. At 16th Street and New York Avenue, the jalopy gave a groan and appeared to breathe its last. There we were — my eight-and-a-half-month pregnant wife, a useless car, and me. The only thing I know less about than cars is delivering babies so I was not feeling very good about the situation. A few hours passed, and we found ourselves in the midst of the celebrants returning from the gala fireworks.

At that point, a Jamaican fellow from Brooklyn got out of his car and asked us if we could use some help. Fortunately, he turned out to be a car mechanic, and, even better, he happened to be carrying what looked like a full service station in his car trunk. He fixed the car, and at 2:00 a.m. we limped back into Baltimore.

Even today my wife occasionally brings up this man's extraordinary kindness to us. Such gratitude is not so hard; an unknown stranger whom we will never see again does not threaten our sense of ourselves in the same way as someone with whom we are in constant contact, and to whom the debt is not only ongoing but incapable of every being repaid.

So how do we protect our self-image and avoid feeling beholden? We act as if whatever we received was something to which we were entitled. "The world owes me" is the national anthem of the yuppie generation. But this psychological trick did not start in the '80s. Already in *Midrash Koheles*, we learn that the natural human instinct is to look at a gift as something to which we were entitled. The *Midrash* relates that there was a certain doctor who knew the Divine Name and all its secret powers. He wanted to bequeath his knowledge to someone, but he had to be sure that person would not abuse his knowledge. Finally, he heard of a *tzaddik* named Rav Pinchos ben Chama, who was worthy of this esoteric knowledge.

But before the doctor would pass on his wisdom, he asked Rav Pinchos ben Chama one question: "Have you ever received a favor from anyone?" And when Rav Pinchos ben Chama answered that he had once received something from someone, the doctor told him that he was disqualified from knowing the

Divine Name. If you once received something from someone else, the doctor explained, you view it as yours by right, and I can no longer trust you with my gift. If someone refuses to do a favor for you one day, you might become enraged and use the Divine Name in anger. From this *Midrash* we see how hard it is to show *hakaras hatov,* and particularly to our parents.

The respect necessary to ensure the proper transmission of the *mesorah* is also difficult for us. Human beings do not like to accept authority, to be told what to do. Each of us wants to be his own boss, the one setting the rules. And this natural inclination to rebel against authority has been exacerbated to the highest degree today. The *Gemara* at the end of *Sotah* tells us that in the era preceding the advent of *Mashiach* — and that is the period in which we are living today — *chutzpah* and insolence will be triumphant. The young will humiliate their elders, and the elders will rise before the young.

This general trend is intensified by our democratic, egalitarian society, and the truth is that I am a believer in democracy compared to any of the other alternatives available today. But democracy has its costs, one of which is that the whole concept of authority is an alien one in our society. The credo of our society is: "Don't tell me what to do. My opinion is as valid as yours." There are no institutions or people in America today that command unusual respect.

Those who grow up in authoritarian societies, in which the ruler commands absolute obedience, have much less difficulty showing their parents respect. An Iranian young man once told me that it would never have occurred to him as a child to pass his father or mother anything with only one hand. Everything had to be given to a parent with two hands as a token of respect. Today if we ask our children for something, we are as likely as not to be told, "Hey, Dad, it's over there." Forget about two hands, forget about one hand.

I remember once being in the *beis medrash* on a Friday night when a rabbi from Iran was reunited with his sons after many years. As the sons came over to him after *davening*, their father extended his hand for each one — from the oldest to the youngest — to kiss. You just do not see that kind of respect in America today.

The truth is that we are partly to blame for the situation. We simply do not teach our children how to respect a parent, and then we are surprised when they do not show any respect. The halachah is that a child should stand when his parents enter the room, but how many of us insist on that? We are so eager to show that we are regular guys that our children would be amazed to learn such a mitzvah even exists. They would be equally amazed to learn that one is not supposed to interrupt his parents, even to agree with them.

Another reason our children do not learn respect is that we have not provided them with proper models. Do they see *us* showing respect by subordinating our judgment to that of someone wiser than us? Do they see us honoring our own parents as is fitting?

We teach our children Torah and *chesed,* but we do not teach them how to respect their parents. There is a place for just sitting down on the couch and giving your children the opportunity to serve you for no other reason than that you are their parent. Instead we serve them as drivers of one car pool after another.

Of course, this can be taken too far. A parent should never take advantage of his position in order to place unnecessary burdens on children; this would certainly not engender respect. Nor can we be too overbearing. The maidservant of Rabi once saw a man striking an older child and said that he should be put in *cherem* for *lifnei iver,* putting a stumbling block in front of his son by causing him to rebel against parental authority. And the *Rambam* writes that it is forbidden to be too strict with one's children (*Hilchos Mamerim* 6:8). But demanding a modicum of respect is not being overbearing. If the halachah states that a child should not sit in your place and should rise for you, there is nothing overbearing about insisting on the halachah. Do not be smarter than the halachah.

⚘KIBUD AV V'EIM AND OUR AGING PARENTS

As modern medicine succeeds in prolonging life, the issue of caring for an aged parent becomes a reality in more and more lives. A *Midrash Hagadol* on the first verse in the Book of *Shemos* — "And these are the names of the children of Israel who were coming to Egypt; *with Yaakov,* each man and his family came" — teaches us of the obligation to take care of our aging parents. Why didn't the verse simply say that these are the names of the children of Israel who came to Egypt with their families? The *Midrash* answers that Yaakov is interjected into the sentence to teach us that even though each of those mentioned was an adult with his own household of dependents, they first attended to the needs of their aging father Yaakov.

The halachah gives some precise guidelines of our obligations to our parents, though much is left open. The expenses of caring for our parents should, whenever possible, be borne by the parent (*Yoreh Deah* 230). The *Rema* adds, however, that when the parent does not have sufficient assets to care for himself then the children can be forced to bear the expenses according to their financial capacities.

One of the most painful questions that many of us have to confront at one time or another with respect to our elderly parents is the issue of whether to have them live with us or in some kind of home for the elderly. Our natural inclination is, of course, to try and keep our parents with us for as long as possible. But that is not always possible for a variety of reasons: lack of space, the parent's need for constant medical attention, or simply the lack of emotional resources on the part of ourselves or our spouses.

There is no question that the burden can sometimes be overwhelming. The *Gemara* in *Kiddushin* describes a situation in which a son provides his father with the finest of delicacies to eat and yet loses his *Olam Haba* for the manner in which he does so. *Tosafos* cites a *Yerushalmi* which gives an example. The son places before his father a plate of fine food, and his father asks him where he obtained the money for such delicacies. Instead of answering the question, the son tells his father, "What do you care? Eat."

Commenting on this *Gemara*, Rabbi Reuven Feinstein focused on the psychology that could explain such great solicitude for the parent on the one hand, and such cruelty on the other hand. What happened, he suggests, is that the son spent far beyond his means out of his sense of obligation to his father, but then he resented his father for putting him in a position where he felt obligated to spend so much. Such an admixture of obligation and resentment is almost always present to one degree or another. But we do not wish to reach a situation in which the child feels he must have his parent live with him at all costs but is unable to hide or restrain his bitterness at the situation. In such a case, keeping his parent in his home is completely counterproductive. The last thing an elderly parent wants is to feel that he is a burden or to have the love he showered on his children requited in his old age with resentment. The *Shulchan Aruch* (*Yoreh Deah* 240:10) specifically says that in a case where the parent has become senile or demented, and the situation is impossible for the child, he should find others to handle the day to day care.

Recently there was a study done by some researchers at the University of Michigan, and they found that loneliness is the single greatest threat to the health of an elderly person — greater than smoking, high blood pressure, cholesterol, or obesity. So wherever your parents are, don't let them be lonely. Maintain physical and emotional contact.

My father's mother lived with us for many years when I was a boy. Even when she became so infirm that she had to be placed in a home, my father went to visit her every single night for 30 or 40 minutes. Sometimes I accompanied him, and I was never sure that my grandmother knew who I was or even who my father was, but still he kept up that contact every day.

Allow your parents, to the maximum extent possible, to maintain control over their lives. Even where you think their decisions are questionable, do not be quick to take away their ability to make those decisions, to sign their checks — in short to let them control as much of their own lives as possible.

Everyone needs to feel needed, and that need is even greater when one is old and suspects that he or she is just a burden. Parents have a function to perform in our lives that no one else can, and they should be made aware of this. When your baby cuts his first tooth, only the baby, you, and your mother take profound delight in this milestone, so don't forget to let your mother share in this. Share your accomplishments and those of your children with your parents. Take advantage of their experience and consult with them on problems they have been through themselves.

To invert the old saw: Where there is hope there is life; where there is no feeling of a future there is no life. Make your parents look forward to the future — whether it's a grandchild's *bar* mitzvah or wedding, the next holiday, or their next birthday. Dr. Yaakov Mermelstein tells of a daughter who was taken aback that her 96-year-old mother for buying a three-year subscription to a magazine. The only thing greater than the mother's wisdom was the daughter's stupidity. The mother was giving herself the message that she was still going to be around at 99 and her daughter went ahead and expressed her skepticism.

When Rabbi Yaakov Kamenetsky was 85, his doctor prescribed a certain medicine for him. Reb Yaakov questioned him about side effects, but the doctor brushed these aside on the grounds that the only side effects were long term and thus irrelevant for anyone his age. Reb Yaakov told him, "What do you mean? I have another thirty-five years," and refused to take the medicine. Past 90, he still expressed the wish at every *bris* that he would be there to celebrate the *bar* mitzvah as well.

Reb Yaakov, in his sharp-mindedness, gave himself a future, and that's what we have to do for our parents. At Chanukah we have to start talking to them about where they will be for Pesach, and at Pesach about whether this is the year that we will finally buy a new *succah*. Give them something to look forward to, something to live for.

~ THE UNFINISHED MISSION

No one can deny that there is often a great deal of pain associated with caring for elderly or sick parents. But nothing is free in this world, and that includes love. Sometimes the price of love is pain. This idea was beautifully expressed by a daughter coming to grips with her mother's increasing infirmity:

> *You bathe and pat dry the bones that once housed you.*
> *You spoon-feed the lips that kissed your cuts and bruises and made them well.*

You comb the hair that used to playfully cascade and make you laugh.

You arrange the covers over the legs that once carried you into the air.

The naps are as frequent as yours used to be.

You accompany her to the bathroom and you wait to return her to her bed.

You never thought it would be like this, but that's the price of love.

As painful as it sometimes is, this is not a duty that we can shirk. It might help us to remember that the *Ribbono shel Olam* repays us measure for measure. The way we treat our parents — and the example we set for our children — is the way our children will treat us. If we fulfill our obligations with a sense of gratitude, respect and love, then we can expect that our children will do the same.

Rabbi Tarfon was extraordinary in the respect he showed his mother. He used to bend over and make himself into a stepstool so that she could climb onto his back to get into bed. And when his mother walked outside, he used to put his hands down for her to step on rather than have her bare feet touch the ground.

Once Rabbi Tarfon was very ill, and his mother sat by his bed praying for his recovery. His colleagues came to visit him, and she begged them to pray for the recovery of a son who showed such great honor to his mother. But even after she told them all that he had done, the Sages only said, "Even if he honored you a thousandfold more, he would still not have fulfilled half his obligation of *kibud av v'eim*."

What kind of friends were these? Shouldn't they have emphasized Rabbi Tarfon's exceptional merit in his time of need in order to arouse Hashem's mercy on him? As a young man, the *Avnei Nezer* of Sochatchov explained that the Sages were indeed emphasizing a trait that *should* earn Rabbi Tarfon heavenly mercy. His mother might have thought that the great Tanna had done everything for which he had been created in the world: He had taught students, his opinions are cited in the *Mishnah*. But the Sages told her: His mission is still not complete. Despite all he has achieved, he still has a task in this world — honoring you. And therefore, he should live.

No matter how great a person is, the Sages told her, as long as his parents are alive, he still has an unfulfilled mission — taking care of and honoring them in the proper way.

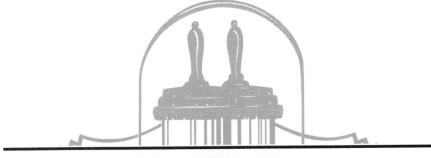

MIDDOS/ PERSONALITY

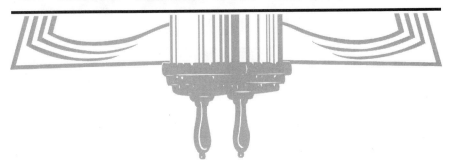

What — Me Angry?
— Never!

The person who has never experienced anger does not exist. Anger, as we shall see, is in large part a function of our frustration when our desires are thwarted, and since there is no person without any desires or who has his or her every whim fulfilled, there is no one who does not have to learn to control his temper.

I hope that I will not be thought to be revealing any secrets if I say that this applies to the greatest *talmidei chachamim* and *tzaddikim* as well as ourselves. We often have the mistaken image of the *Chafetz Chaim* and other *gedolim* as having been born perfect, and that is far from the case. While it may seem a token of our respect that we imagine our *gedolim* in this fashion, we actually diminish them by viewing them in this way, for we thereby ignore the source of their greatness: the decades of intense effort spent working on themselves. At the same time, by imagining the *gedolim* as born perfect, we deprive them of any relevance as models for us in leading our lives. And that is an evasion. Precisely because of the way they worked on themselves are they the best models for us.

Just after World War II, the Shulsinger Shas was published for the first time, and HaRav Moshe Feinstein was one of the first to buy this beautiful new edition of the Vilna Shas. As many of you know, Reb Moshe was a prolific writer, and he used to write in his margins as he learned. In those days, fountain pens were still considered the proper way to write, and Reb Moshe used to sit with an inkwell on his desk from which he would periodically fill his pen. One day when Reb Moshe was away from his *Gemara* for a few moments, one of his closest *talmidim* came over to see what he was writing in the margins. As he leaned over the brand new *Shas*, he accidentally tipped over the inkwell, and a big blue inkblot quickly spread all over the *daf* (page) Reb Moshe was learning and down the side of the *Gemara*. The *talmid* stood there frozen in horror until Reb Moshe returned. Reb Moshe took one look at the *Gemara* and another at the terrified boy and said, "Doesn't the *Gemara* look beautiful in blue?"

Whenever Reb Moshe was asked about the incident subsequently, he always emphasized, "It took me years to learn how to do that. You don't think I had a temper? But I worked on myself constantly, and I learned how to control my temper."

Even the *Chafetz Chaim* got angry. But he taught himself to step back from the situation and repeat to himself, "Yisrael Meir, don't get angry." Whenever that happened he developed the ability, as it were, to turn himself into an objective observer of his own anger and from that vantage point, speak to himself in such a way as to gain control of his anger.

◄◊ GEHINNOM ON EARTH

The *Gemara* says, "An angry person has all forms of *Gehinnom* (Hell) rule over him." Usually this is understood to mean that a person who never learns to control his anger will end up in *Gehinnom*. But Rabbi Yerucham Levovitz, the famous *Mashgiach* of the Mirrer Yeshiva in Poland, understood the *Gemara* as referring to this world. A person who has no control over his anger, who is always exploding and flying off the handle, writes Reb Yerucham, is living a hell on earth. He is out of control, he is not master of his life. Rather he is ruled by everything that happens to him or that somebody does to him.

A person who cannot control his temper may recognize how self-destructive his actions are, but he cannot stop himself. The *Midrash* tells us that the plague of frogs in Egypt started with a single frog. Only when the Egyptians struck the frog did it turn into two, and as they continued hitting the frogs produced in this fashion, they kept splitting and multiplying exponentially.

If the Egyptians saw that every time they struck a frog, they only multiplied more, the Steipler Gaon once asked, why didn't they stop? He answered that they couldn't stop; they were out of control. Once their anger had gotten the best of them, they could not restrain themselves even at the cost of increasing the plague.

～ PRIDE AND ANGER — PARTNERS IN CRIME

The *middah* (trait) of anger is inextricably bound with that of pride. From the first appearance of anger in the Torah through the *Gemara* to the *Rishonim*, this conjunction of pride and anger is taken as a given.

Kayin's anger towards his brother Hevel is the first recorded instance of anger in the Torah: "And Kayin was very angry, and his countenance fell." Kayin was crestfallen when his brother Hevel's sacrifice was accepted by Hashem and his was not, and acting out of that anger, he killed Hevel. The commentators locate Kayin's anger in the threat to his self-image when Hashem rejected his sacrifice in favor of Hevel's. As the *Netziv* puts it:

> Anger brings great suffering that causes the body to become inflamed and the blood to boil. . . a suffering so great that it is close to death. This suffering is brought about because something was done not according to his will . . . and it comes from a prideful heart, from the feeling that such a thing should not have occurred to him due to his importance in his own eyes.

In effect Kayin said to Hashem: What do You mean that my offering is not accepted? How can You accept his offering and not mine? Throw in the natural sibling rivalry, and you find a potent brew of assaults to Kayin's ego, which led directly to his murder of Hevel. Ego — damaged ego, thwarted ego, crushed ego — and the result is anger, even murder.

Most of us do not go as far as Kayin: We have been too socialized for that. But behind every expression of anger, writes Rabbi Moshe Chaim Luzzatto in *Mesillas Yesharim*, lurks the suppressed desire to murder whoever thwarts our will, meaning that anger, when permitted to go to extreme lengths, can result in violence and even bloodshed.

In our anger, we recognize nothing other than our own will. That is why *Chazal* (*Shabbos* 105b) liken one who tears his garment or breaks his vessels in anger to an idol worshiper. His anger and frustration results from a feeling that everything should go as he wants because he is the one calling the shots in the world. It is a reflection of his failure to acknowledge that it is the *Ribbono shel Olam's* world, and it is He who decides if and when something should happen. And that failure to recognize that it is Hashem's world is tantamount to idolatry.

In the opening chapter of *Hilchos Dei'os*, the *Rambam* writes that we should always seek the golden mean with respect to each character trait — tending neither too far in one direction nor the other. Yet in the very next chapter, he writes that there is no middle ground for two traits. The first of these is a haughty heart. It is not enough, writes the *Rambam*, to be modest; one must strive for an extremely lowly spirit. And similarly, the trait of anger is an extremely evil one to which a person should go to any length to avoid. Again we find anger and pride linked together.

The ego problem which leads us to anger is not, as we may at first glance think, an overly high opinion of ourselves, though it is often expressed in that way. In truth, it is rare today to meet someone with a really high opinion of himself — a true *ba'al ga'avah*. Far more common are people of fragile egos, who compensate for their insecurity by putting on a show of bravado. Because their egos are so fragile, they are incapable of dealing with frustration. Every time someone does not do what they want or something does not go as planned, they take this as confirmation of their subconscious view of themselves as inadequate.

Our fragile egos are one of the greatest impediments to successful marriage today. We tend to view our spouses' primary task as massaging our tender egos. When even they disagree with us or do not do something exactly as we want, we take this as the greatest affront of all. After all, why did we marry if not to have someone around to permanently adore us and praise us? Similarly, our children and students have the power to anger us more than anyone else because we view them as obligated to listen to us. If even those under our authority do not jump to our beck and call, we really feel like nothings.

Because our egos are so fragile, we tend to put everything in the context of a personal attack on us or as an expression of contempt. A husband asks his wife in the morning to make a deposit in the bank and tells her that it is very important, as he plans to write several checks that day against that deposit. That night as he walks through the door, his first question is: "Did you remember to make the deposit?" When his wife claps her hand to her head, he explodes.

What is happening here? He feels that if his wife really loved him, if she respected him, that deposit would have been the most important item of her day's agenda. Her failure to make the deposit, then, is not simple forgetfulness, but a reflection of the fact that she does not love him.

If we analyze all those occasions when we lose our tempers, we will see how many of them have to do with affronts to our pride. You go into the dry cleaner and put down $20 for an $8 bill, and the dry cleaner gives you two dollars in change. You may explode with anger. Why? Because you think that he thinks you are an idiot. You may tell yourself that it's the principle involved: You hate cheating. But if you reflect on that for a moment, you will realize that when your friend tells you about a similar incident that happened to him, it does not make your blood boil quite in the same way. Why not? Because when it happens to your friend, no one was taking *you* for a fool — and you knew immediately that the proprietor had made an honest mistake.

When we realize that the reason we are losing our temper is that our egos are somehow being threatened, it gives us a chance to get that temper under control. It is possible my wife did not make the deposit because she was not paying attention to what I said. But is it not more likely that she had an extremely hectic day and just forgot under the pressure of a hundred things to do? Maybe my students are not paying attention today because they have little respect for my knowledge, but it is at least as likely that they are preoccupied with their test schedules or some major sports event. Maybe my children do not jump to do everything I ask them immediately because they do not love or respect me. But could it not be that they are too engrossed in the book they are reading to have heard what I said? And did the dry cleaner really single me out to short-change me because he thinks I am stupid, or does he try that on everyone? Or could he have made an innocent mistake?

❧ ANGER AND THE YERUSHALMI KUGELS

An incident that took place in the Frand household the last *Erev Shabbos* before Rosh Hashanah illustrates many of these principles. My wife wanted to go to the mall to buy my daughter a dress for *Yom Tov,* but my son and I needed the car for various errands. "No problem," I told my wife, "I'll drop you off at the mall and pick you up at 4:00, and you'll have plenty of time before Shabbos."

Now my plan was fine as far as it went, and had everything gone smoothly, everybody would have been perfectly happy. Unfortunately, however, we were not operating with an unlimited margin of error, for in addition to the usual pre-Shabbos preparations, my wife was in the process of making several *Yerushalmi kugels* — *Yerushalmi kugels* for a close friend's *simchah, Yerushalmi kugels* for Shabbos, *Yerushalmi kugels* for Rosh Hashanah. Everywhere the eye could see, the kitchen was covered with *Yerushalmi kugel* batter. True, all that was left to do was to put the eggs in the batter and pop the *kugels* into the oven, but to do that you have to be home, and therein lay the rub.

As four o'clock drew near, I realized that I was running late, and I called my son Yaakov to go pick up his mother and sister. But when I arrived home at 4:35, there was still no Yaakov, no wife, no Avigayil to be found. To make matters worse, my other son Baruch informed me that my wife had just called to say she had been waiting a half an hour. After waiting ten minutes for the happy family to return home, I decided that I had better hop back in the car and head up to the mall. On my way, I happened to glance over into the approaching lane of traffic and who should I see but my son Yaakov. A closer inspection of the car, however, revealed no other members of the Frand clan. "What could have gone wrong?" I asked myself.

As I arrived at the mall it finally hit me that I had been something less than very wise. Macy's has several entrances, and I had forgotten to tell Yaakov which one to go to. Actually it was worse than that: I could not remember myself where I had dropped off my wife or where I told her to wait. By this time, Shabbos was less than an hour away, and the kitchen was still awash in *Yerushalmi kugel* batter.

I went to one entrance, and my wife wasn't there. I pulled up to the second entrance and still no wife. After repeating this scene a few more times, I had no choice but to go into the mall. I called home, and the worst was confirmed: "Mommy just called and she's been waiting over an hour." I did, however, gain one crucial piece of information while inside the mall: There is a third entrance. The stranger from whom I extracted this information seemed surprised that the question of whether Macy's has another entrance could have caused such a frantic look on my face.

Close to 5:30, I finally pulled up to the right entrance. I braced myself, since we can all recognize that this is one of those classic delicate scenarios. As my wife entered the car, a profusion of apologies for my stupidity poured trippingly off my tongue. My wife simply said, "It's O.K." and that was that.

How did she do it? How did she keep from working herself to such a boil that by the time I got there no apology could have kept her from venting her pent-up anger? The answer is that she did not view my tardiness as an assault on her ego, as an expression of my lack of concern for her. Nor did she confuse stupidity with insensitivity. She had time to *think* and mentally prepare her response. That makes all the difference.

But there is more to this story, and my wife insists that I also share this next episode so that no one should prematurely recommend her for induction into the Hall of Fame of the Most Righteous. I was, by this time, full of good resolutions. Though I had been determined to be prompt for *Minchah* this last Shabbos of the year, I decided that my first responsibility was making sure that my wife did not have to share her kitchen that Shabbos with the *Yerushalmi kugel* batter. But I had a problem. I had to pick up my other son's suit at the cleaners. If I took my wife home first, I'd never have time to run out again, pick up the suit, and still help in the kitchen.

I did not, however, share any of my altruistic calculations with my wife, and as we headed home, I turned in to pick up the dry cleaning. My wife was a little stunned to find that with Shabbos now half an hour away we were still not going straight home. Suffice it to say that the first words out of her mouth were not, "How nice, dear, that you have thought of another mitzvah to do *Erev Shabbos.*" By not telling her what I was going to do and why, I had made it that much harder for her to convince herself that she was not married to the world's most insensitive clod, who after having kept her waiting for an hour and a half and with Shabbos fast upon us had unilaterally decided that the dry cleaning took precedence over getting home.

◆ SOME TIPS ON CONTROLLING ANGER

From all that we've said, it is clear that the first question that we have to ask ourselves when we feel anger coming on is: Why am I angry? Is this just a matter of my ego being too large or too fragile? If that does not work, try asking yourself: Is it worth getting angry about? One clue to whether something is worth being angry about *now* is whether you will still be angry about it in two days. If not, why not just save yourself the two days and forget it. Anger destroys all that we value most highly — our marriages, our relations with our children.

We have to train ourselves to remember that most of what we place so much importance on is simply not worthy of our concern. As the *Rambam* writes at the end of *Hilchos Dei'os* (7:7): "[A Jew] should always be prepared to ignore the slights and offenses of others. These are nothing but vanity and emptiness, and they are not worth our taking revenge."

I once spoke in Philadelphia about this subject, and after my speech a man approached me and shared with me how he had come to learn that there is very little worth losing one's temper about. A little over a year earlier, he had been at a *bar* mitzvah and started to feel ill, and he requested someone else there to drive him home. As they were driving home, he asked his driver to take him to the nearest hospital instead. His sense that he was in bad shape was soon confirmed. He had a type of aneurysm from which about one in ten survive. Since then, he told me, all those things that used to drive him mad no longer bother him at all. He's just happy to be alive, and everything else is just so much nonsense. It is all a matter of perspective.

Another insight that can help us evaluate whether something is worth getting angry about: Winston Churchill once said that one can judge the stature of a person by those things that anger him. The smaller the person, the greater the number of trivialities that cause him to lose control. And the more elevated the person, the fewer things that can cause him to grow angry. Do we want to think of ourselves as people whose lives are soured by the way the toothpaste tube is squeezed?

Sometimes none of these suggested questions can spare us from losing our temper. Fire prevention has failed. How can we douse the flames? The cardinal rule here is: If you cannot stifle your anger, at least delay its expression. Don't react immediately. Rabbeinu Yehudah Hachassid writes in *Sefer HaChassidim* of a certain man who gave his son one piece of advice on his deathbed: Sleep on your anger. When that son grew up, he married, and then he left on a long journey that took him away from home for many years. After all those years, he returned home and found his wife embracing a young man. He was about to pull out his sword and kill both of them when he remembered his father's advice to sleep on his anger. The next morning he learned that the young man was his own son.

Rabbi Elya Lopian once waited two weeks to speak with his son after the latter had angered him. He wanted to make sure it was he speaking, and not his anger. The Alter of Kelm used to have a special coat that he called his *beged haka'as* (literally, his garment of anger). Whenever he was angry, he went to the closet and put on this garment. By the time he had put it on, he had already cooled off. A Chassidic Rebbe had a magic cure for problems of *shalom bayis* (marital harmony). He would give the feuding couple bottles of "holy water" and tell them to fill their mouths with this "holy water" and keep it there for a while whenever they felt themselves growing angry.

If you can't hold in your anger, try going to another room before exploding. While there, look in the mirror. The sight of how ridiculous you look in a state of apoplexy may well help you to regain control.

Sometimes the problem is that our anger has become so habitual and undifferentiated that we are no longer even aware of it. Here the first task is resensitizing ourselves to our own actions. We once noticed in the Frand household that the decibel level had grown too high. To ensure that shouting did not come to seem like the normal form of speech, we instituted a system of nickel fines for hollering. The fines didn't break anyone's piggy bank, but they did have the salutary effect of making us conscious of undesirable reaction patterns that had developed over time.

We have been discussing how to control our anger after we have already experienced those initial feelings of irritation. But is there anything that we can do to prevent those feelings from arising in the first place?

One thing we can do is to work on acquiring the trait of patience. A patient person is one who recognizes that the whole world does not operate according to his or her time clock, that it is *Hakadosh Boruch Hu,* and not he, who determines when something is going to happen. A person who can recognize this has gone a long way towards forestalling anger.

Patience can only be acquired patiently. There is no way to go about transforming ourselves into patient people other than one step at a time. In this respect, becoming a patient person is like training oneself to not speak *lashon hara:* It must be done step by step. Just as people begin by setting aside specific hours that they will not speak *lashon hara,* so we can work on being patient by beginning with specific hours during which we concentrate on not letting things bother us.

If we can succeed in sensitizing ourselves to the need for patience in one area of our lives, this will gradually spill over into other areas as well. One situation that triggers my own impatience is being stuck behind someone trying to make a left turn. I am often irritated over the timidity of the driver in front of me, and I am as likely as not to whip into the right lane to get around him and then move back over to the left. But I am trying to teach myself to look at the time stuck in the left lane as character building. My children are even authorized when they see this little end-around maneuver to remind me that I am working on becoming a patient driver.

Obviously the first place we have to learn to be patient is in the home with our spouses and children. Rabbi Shlomo Wolbe points out that the word for marriage — *nissuin* — means to carry. There are certain things about our spouse that will always be a burden for us, and we have to learn to carry this burden. We can always hope that our spouses will change those things that irritate us, but we should not live in the expectation that they will. We have to be prepared to live with the fact that certain things about our spouses will always be difficult for us, and the same goes for our children. We are not perfect, and have no right to demand perfection of them.

Above all, we have to learn a little patience with ourselves. Just because we resolve to do better in those areas in which we recognize the need for improvement in our calmer moments does not mean that it is going to happen overnight. As the verse tells us, "A *tzaddik* falls seven times and rises" (Mishlei 24:16). The difference between the righteous person and the wicked one lies not in the falling, but in whether he gets back up again. We have to remember this and not allow every failure to control our tempers to mark us in our own eyes for life as an angry person.

✒ IS IT EVER PERMISSIBLE TO GET ANGRY?

As parents we have the responsibility of raising our children to follow a certain path. Part of discharging that responsibility is making our children understand that certain behavior is beyond the pale and cannot be tolerated. If we fail to inculcate this lesson when they are young, it will come back to haunt us later. But even here, where it is permissible to show anger for the purpose of teaching our children, the operative word is *show* anger. Our anger, writes Rabbi Moshe Chaim Luzzatto in *Mesillas Yesharim,* must be anger of the face, not anger in the heart. Our children sense the difference too. If they see that we are out of control, our anger is likely to leave them with a far different lesson than we intended: that it is permissible to lose our tempers, or at least that it is permissible when you grow older and are a parent.

It is also permissible to hate someone who causes Hashem's Name and Torah to be desecrated in the world, but that has little to do with the anger that we have been discussing and which destroys our lives. Here, too, caution is in order. We should not be too quick to justify our anger as *leshem Shomayim* (for the sake of Heaven). Some of the *ba'alei mussar* have explained the statement in *Pirkei Avos,* that an argument for the sake of Heaven has permanence, to mean that when the parties convince themselves that they are acting for the sake of Heaven theirs is an argument to which there will be no end.

Finally, there are those instances in which people do such terrible things that it is beyond the normal human capacity to forgive, e.g., a woman deserted by her husband and left an *agunah. Sefer HaChinuch* tells us that a person is not expected to be so devoid of feeling as not to react to such hurt: He "should not be as if dead and without feelings." But no matter how understandable and justified our anger, we gain nothing by nurturing it. Rarely does our anger have any affect on those who have hurt us — at most it gives us one more grievance against them. If we let our anger — even justified anger — control us, we are the only ones who lose. It is our lives which become not worth living.

As Jews, our definition of a mighty man is not one of great physical strength but one who controls his emotions: "One who is slow to anger is greater than a mighty man, and one who

rules over his passions is greater than the conqueror of cities."
No quality causes us to gain more favor with Hashem than
accepting insult without responding. When we do so, we fulfill
the mitzvah to emulate Hashem, Who created the world through
an act of self-restraint and contraction and who spares us each
moment by refraining from judging us according to Strict
Judgment. Those who exercise self-control and refrain from
anger are the true heroes who give satisfaction to their Creator.

The Concept
of Tznius

L et me begin by dispelling two common myths with respect to *tznius*. The first of these is that *tznius* is a concept that applies exclusively to women, and the second is that *tznius* is primarily an issue of sleeve lengths and hemlines.

A quick examination of the instances in which a variant of the Hebrew root צנע, denoting something hidden or private, appears in *Tanach* or is used by *Chazal* will quickly reveal that *tznius*, the requirement of conducting oneself modestly, is equally incumbent upon men and women. *Klal Yisrael* is compared to a dove. As *Chazal* say, "Just as the dove is a modest bird, so are the children of Israel modest." Note that *Chazal* did not compare the dove to Jewish women but to all Jews. We find in the Book of Mishlei (11:2) the verse ואת צנועים חכמה — "Those who are private will achieve wisdom." *Chazal* interpret this to mean that those who learn intensely in private will not quickly forget their learning. How many women can be described as poring over a page of *Gemara*? Obviously *Chazal* are talking here about men. Similarly, in *Derech Eretz Zutra* (7), we are told that a Torah scholar must be extremely modest in his dress. Furthermore, one who teaches words of Torah in public is enjoined to be as modest as a *kallah*.

So much for the myth that *tznius* is relevant only to women. Now for the second myth that *tznius* is primarily an issue of the length of one's sleeves and hems. The most famous verse in *Tanach* in which the root צנע appears is that at the end of the Book of Michah (6:8): "He has told you, man, what is good and what the L-rd seeks from you, only to act justly, love *chesed*, and walk modestly (והצנע לכת) before your L-rd." Clearly, when the prophet describes walking modestly as one of the three cardinal principles by which every Jew must guide his life, he is describing a concept far more encompassing than the appropriate styles in women's dress.

Indeed the *Gemara* (*Makkos* 24a) gives two situations included in this injunction when one must be especially modest: at a funeral and at a wedding. In both cases, walking modestly implies not calling attention to oneself either by weeping uncontrollably at a funeral or by making oneself the focus of attention at a wedding. *Chazal* were not warning us that on these two occasions women must be more careful with respect to their dress, but that diverting attention to oneself deflects the thoughts of those present from what they should be focused on: the loss of the deceased in the case of the funeral and on rejoicing with the groom and bride in the case of the wedding.

Because Rachel *Imeinu* excelled in the trait of modesty, we are told, she merited that her descendant Shaul also excelled in this *middah*. *Chazal* are not referring to the fact that Rachel wore ankle-length dresses and a kerchief pulled down to her eyebrows, but rather to the discreet signs that she and Yaakov developed to communicate with one another on their wedding night. Nor did Shaul distinguish himself by the length of his tunic but rather by his extreme privacy. Even in times of war, he would never relieve himself in an open field, but always waited until he could find a cave or other hidden place.

A CALL TO THE INNER BEING

Thus far we have defined *tznius* negatively — i.e., in terms of what it is not. It is now time for us to try to give the concept a more positive definition. *Tznius*, in fact, encompasses a number of closely related ideas. Above all, it is a call to us to emphasize and strengthen the internal aspects of our personality, to concentrate our energies on that which is deeper and more hidden within us — our spiritual nature. That is why the command to walk humbly before G-d could serve for the prophet Michah as one of the three basic principles upon which a Jew must conduct his life. It is nothing less than a demand that we emphasize the Divine image within us, the soul which was taken from under the *Kisei HaKavod* (Divine throne) and brought into the physical world.

The specific laws concerning proper attire and the like are expressions of this overriding command. Their purpose is to ensure that our attention is not diverted by the beauty of the physical body from the spiritual being that constitutes the essence of others as well as ourselves.

Walking humbly before G-d can also be understood as walking privately before Him. To fulfill the command, then, is to guide our behavior solely according to the recognition that our every act is in the presence of G-d. Thus whether we are in our inner sanctum or in a crowd of people is irrelevant, for there is ultimately only one Judge of our actions, and His is the only approval we seek.

This attitude radically distinguishes us from the prevailing society for whose members the approval of others is the only source of validation. We live today in what might be termed a public relations society. If an event is not recorded in the media, it is as if it did not occur at all. Many celebrities employ publicity agents whose sole task is to ensure that their client's name appears as frequently as possible in newspapers and magazines so that others will know that he or she is still important.

By contrast, the most crucial moments in Jewish history were often those that took place in absolute solitude, as far from the eyes of the world as possible. We as a people take our name, Yisrael, from Yaakov's encounter with an angel. The Torah's account of the event begins, "And Yaakov was left alone... " (Bereishis 32:25). Yaakov's being by himself of necessity preceded his grappling with the angel. And when the angel tells Yaakov that he will henceforth be known as Yisrael, he explains, "for you have striven with the Divine and with man and you have prevailed" (Bereishis 32:29). Rabbi Moshe Meiselman, in *Jewish Women in Jewish Law*, however, notes that Onkelos makes a crucial change in preposition — so that the verse reads "you have fought before G-d and against man." In other words, the only audience to whom Yaakov attached any importance was G-d Himself, and this is reflected in the name Yisrael passed down to his descendants throughout the generations.

From a modern, "public relations" perspective, Akeidas Yitzchak was a gigantic missed opportunity. No reporters of any kind were there. Yet it is the very solitude of the drama that the Torah stresses. Avraham and Yitzchak's ascent to Har HaMoriah was preceded by telling Yishmael and Eliezer, who had accompanied them on the early stages of the journey, that they must remain behind.

Over and over, the Torah emphasizes the solitude in which the pivotal events in the moral history of the Jewish people occurred. Thus Yosef's temptation took place when "no member of the household was there in the house" (Bereishis 39:11). It was the vision of his father Yaakov's face, representing the Divine imperative, that spared him at that moment when all those forces and instincts the world calls "natural" militated in favor of sin.

Though all of *Klal Yisrael* heard Hashem speak at Sinai, Moshe *Rabbeinu* received the details of the Torah in the course of forty days alone on the mountain with only Hashem as his teacher. Jewish ritual also captures the fact that the essential confrontation in every Jew's life is between him and G-d alone. Thus when the Temple stands, the epiphany of the holiest day of the year, Yom Kippur, is the Kohen Gadol's entrance into the Holy of Holies. At that moment, "no man may be in the Tent of Assembly from when he comes to atone in the Holy Place until he leaves" (VaYikra 16:17).

WHY WOMEN ARE SINGLED OUT

Though we have established that the command to walk humbly before G-d (הצנע לכת) is one of the highest religious virtues for both men and women, it remains true that one never hears of lectures being given to men on the topic of *tznius*. Nor is men's attire often the subject of halachic discussion.

This emphasis on *tznius* as it concerns women is not accidental. *Chazal* themselves make clear that there is some unique aspect of a woman's personality that requires the development of the quality of modesty to a deeper level than in a man. We are taught, for instance, that Chavah was created from Adam's rib in order that she and her descendants would be endowed with the quality of *tznius*. To that end, Hashem chose a part of Adam's body that lies beneath the skin and is normally covered by clothing.

All Jews are enjoined to be basically private beings, whose focus is on their inner life, but women are encouraged to a much greater degree than men to shun the public sphere. That is the meaning of the words a Jewish woman hears repeatedly from the time she is a little girl: "The entire glory of the king's daughter lies on the inside" (Mishlei 45:14).

I have a theory — and it is no more than that — as to why *Chazal* placed such emphasis on a woman's development of this quality of *tznius*. It would seem to me that a woman's *tznius* is the protective shell for the *binah* (understanding) that *Chazal* tell us she is blessed with in extra measure. *Binah* is a mental-emotional quality that gives a woman an intuitive grasp of certain matters, an ability to see beneath the surface of people or situations and penetrate to their essence. Women are by nature more empathetic than men; they are quicker to relate to others on an emotional level that goes past the superficialities of social rituals.

I am confident that all of us could quickly come up with numerous instances of how a woman's intuitive grasp saved the day. I'll just share two cases about which I know personally that come immediately to mind. The first involves a woman who happened to be sitting at the table when someone made a business proposition to her husband. She immediately sensed that there was something not quite right about this fellow and ended up saving her husband from a con man. The second case concerns a young couple who were seeing each other. The boy made an excellent impression, and the girl was very enthusiastic about the prospect. Her mother, however, was sure that something was not right with the boy, and over her daughter's vehement protests stopped the match. As subsequent events proved, she thereby saved her daughter from a disastrous marriage.

Yet while a woman is naturally endowed with more *binah* than a man, *binah*, like all natural abilities, has to be nurtured. That is where a woman's special connection to *tznius* comes in. If a woman does not develop her inner self, if she dresses in a manner to attract attention to her physical beauty and that beauty becomes the focus of her concern, her natural intuition will wither and die, for she will have turned herself into a superficial person in denial of her true nature.

The highest level of *binah* found in the Torah is that of Sarah *Imeinu*. It was she who observed Yishmael playing and intuitively knew that he threatened the very continuity of *Klal Yisrael*, which Avraham had been promised would be through her son Yitzchak. Avraham initially rejected her counsel to banish Yishmael from his home. As a father, Avraham could not bring himself to take such a harsh step until Hashem told him, "Whatever Sarah tells you, heed her voice. . ." (Bereishis 21:12). From this statement, *Chazal* learn that Sarah's level of prophecy exceeded that of Avraham (Rashi ad loc.).

Shortly before the events demonstrating Sarah's superiority over Avraham in her ability to evaluate people, the Torah, not coincidentally, emphasizes her *tznius*. When the three angels visit Avraham to inform him of Yitzchak's impending birth, they make a special point of asking Avraham, "Where is Sarah, your wife?" They did so to force Avraham to recognize how exalted she was in the quality of *tznius* — for she had remained out of sight in the tent — and thus endear her even more to him.

The same type of insight shown by Sarah was also found in Rachel, the wife of Rabbi Akiva. Until the age of forty, Rabbi

Akiva was an illiterate and untutored shepherd for Rachel's father, Kalba Savua. So far was he from learning Torah that he later said about himself that before he began to learn he felt such animosity towards Torah scholars that whenever he saw one he wanted to bite him like a donkey. Yet somehow Rachel recognized the vast potential that would one day cause Rabbi Akiva to be recognized as the greatest of the sages of the Talmud, and she defied her father in order to marry him, even at the cost of her entire inheritance. And again, as in the case of Sarah, the Talmud connects her remarkable ability to penetrate beneath Akiva's surface appearance and recognize the potential scholar within to the fact that she excelled in modesty.

✍ OF HEMLINES AND SHIRTSLEEVES AGAIN

We began by proving that *tznius* encompasses far more than the issue of women's attire. And even within that narrow realm, a scrupulous regard for the length of one's hemlines is hardly sufficient to guarantee *tznius*. The woman who walks into her dressmaker and tells her that she wants a long dress, with a high neck, but tight and alluring, has failed to grasp what *tznius* is about.

Just as *tznius* demands of us that we focus on the development of our inner spiritual selves at the expense of the external and superficial, so too does a fulfillment of the mitzvah of *tznius* require that we go beyond a superficial understanding of the concept. My children have a tape that contains an amusing parody of today's Orthodox weddings. A man about to marry off his first daughter calls a professional wedding consultant for advice. First, the consultant tells him that giving each guest a *bentcher* is passé, and suggests a set of *Shas* instead. Though the wedding is in July, he insists that a fur for the mother of the bride is *de rigueur*. Flowers must be picked that day in Holland and flown in on a Concorde, and the Viennese table should leave the guests with their tongues hanging out and making vows to push off the start of their diets until tomorrow.

As the consultant stops to draw his breath, the father of the bride interjects that he wants a modest affair. "You want modesty," the consultant responds without missing a beat. "No problem. On the invitation we'll write: Women should dress in accordance with Orthodox tradition." That, needless to say, is not modesty. *Tznius* is not trying to make others drool with envy so that you will be the talk of the town for weeks no matter how one dresses.

So clearly there is a lot more to *tznius* than long hems and sleeves. But that is not to denigrate the importance of scrupulously observing the halachic standards in dress. Ten years ago, the clothes worn by some Orthodox women may have flirted with the outer limits of the halachically acceptable. Today they are frequently over the line according to all respected opinion.

The feminists were certainly right about one thing. We live in a society that tends to objectify women and evaluate them primarily in terms of their physical beauty. The requirements of modest dress convey, in this context, an important message to both the wearer and to all those with whom she comes into contact. They are a signal to those who see her that she is a human being, which is to say a spiritual being, whose physical body is no more than an outer covering. The secular world does not understand this concept; it accuses Orthodox men who avoid looking at woman of holding them in contempt — but the opposite is actually the case. Precisely because of the laws of *tznius*, Orthodox men are able to look at a woman as a person and not an object. And to the woman herself, dressing in a proper fashion is a constant reminder that her energies are properly focused on the development of the spiritual side of her being.

And finally, dressing in a modest fashion is closely related to the command to be a holy people. Holiness was not meant to be the province of the Jews of Bnei Brak and Jerusalem. We are all commanded to be a holy people and a nation of priests. When we strive for this degree of holiness, when we strive to separate ourselves from the material world, then Hashem can dwell among us, for we have created an environment of holiness conducive to His presence. That is what the verse tells us: "Hashem walks in the midst of your encampment. . ." ((Devarim 23:15). But when is that? Only when He does not see among you any "shameful thing." Because when He sees that He turns away from us.

When Hashem is in our midst, He rescues us and delivers us from our enemies. If we allowed him to dwell in our midst, there would be fewer tragedies and *Eretz Yisrael* would not be imperiled by her enemies within and without. All this depends on *Hakadosh Boruch Hu's* protective shield. Let us take care not to cause it to depart even further from us.

The Roots of
Lashon Hara

Perhaps no mitzvah is the object of so much public concern today as that of proper speech. Nearly a hundred years ago the *Chafetz Chaim* wrote a monumental work of the same name dealing with the laws of *lashon hara*. His intent was to bring the mitzvah of proper speech to the forefront of the consciousness of every religious Jew. But it took many years before the *Chafetz Chaim's* vision was realized. I recall growing up with some general awareness that there was such a thing as *lashon hara*, but it was not a mitzvah that was talked about a great deal.

If today proper speech is the subject of annual gatherings from coast to coast in America, if there are whole days of *shiurim* dedicated to its study in Jerusalem, and, most importantly, if the level of observance of the laws of proper speech has risen dramatically, it is due to the combined efforts of many people building on the pioneering work of the *Chafetz Chaim*: among them Rabbi Yehuda Zev Segal, the Manchester *Rosh Yeshiva*; the *tzadeikes* Chedva Silberfarb, who used the tragic circumstances surrounding her passing at the age of twenty-seven to arouse women all over the world; the organizers of the annual *Yom Iyun* in Jerusalem; and the Chafetz Chaim Heritage Foundation in America.

This concern with speech is one of the defining characteristics of *Am Yisrael*. When *ba'alei teshuvah* are asked what was the first thing that attracted them to becoming religious, a very large number mention the laws of *lashon hara* first. It was these laws that helped them recognize how the Torah aims at the refinement of a human being to a degree beyond anything dreamed of by any other society. Just try telling someone who is not familiar with the laws of *lashon hara* and you will see their mouths drop. What they view as innocuous is for us forbidden; what is commonplace in the speech of every other society will render one a misfit and outcast in a Torah community.

I was once on a plane sitting next to two people who worked in the same office. In the course of the flight, I heard an earful of office politics and a complete psychological dissection of everybody in the office. Listening to the nonstop *lashon hara,* I realized how long it had been since I had heard such talk. It just does not happen anymore in our world. It is socially unacceptable to gossip in such a vulgar fashion.

Of course we have not licked the problem of *lashon hara*. If we had, we would no longer need annual days of introspection concerning this mitzvah around the world. But the existence of those days demonstrates clearly the unique nature of the Jewish people. What other people has placed the refinement of speech at the very top of its agenda? Thousands around the world might demonstrate for or against abortion, for or against capital punishment, but try to imagine any other people drawing tens of thousands — constituting a large percentage of the total Orthodox population — to rallies and speeches devoted to the subject of proper speech. Ask a group of non-Jews to list the greatest problems confronting our society and not one would mention the quality of private speech. As an issue, speech is not even on the agenda.

๛ AN UNCOMPLETED TASK

Think back for a moment to February 2, 1991. (I use the gentile date because it is easier to obtain information from your local library using that date, in case you wish to jog your memory, than it is using 28 *Shevat,* 5751.) Saddam Hussein launched a SCUD missile attack on Israel in which no one was injured and there was only slight property damage. That same day, Secretary of Defense Richard Cheney and Chairman of the Joint Chiefs of Staff Colin Powell arrived in Saudia Arabia to prepare for a ground offensive against Iraqi forces in Kuwait. The air of anticipation was almost unbearable, and there were many among us, myself included, who had the feeling that *Mashiach* was coming.

Our premonitions, we now know, were wrong. *Mashiach* did not come. We witnessed open miracles; the stage was set for *Mashiach;* but he did not come. And in that failure to appear lies the proof that for all our progress in this regard, we have still not cured the outward manifestation of *sinas chinam* (causeless hatred) — i.e., *lashon hara* — that is at the root of our ongoing exile.

At the end of *II Shmuel,* a man named Tziva tells King David that his master Mephibosheth, a son of Saul, has joined Avshalom's rebellion against David. Upon King David's return, Mephibosheth goes to meet him, and ardently denies Tziva's slander. Unable to decide whom to believe, and incapable of disregarding entirely what Tziva has told him, King David tells Mephibosheth, "You and Tziva divide up the estate" (*II Shmuel* 19:30). In that command to divide up (תחלקו) the estate, *Chazal* (*Shabbos* 56) locate the cause for the division of David's kingdom into the kingdoms of Yehudah and Israel. Had King David not credited the *lashon hara* against Mephibosheth, the *Gemara* tells us, King David's kingdom would have remained undivided, the people would never have come to worship idols, and we would not have been exiled from our Land.

The *Maharal* writes in *Nesivos Olam* that the reason for our prolonged exile is *lashon hara,* and echoing him, the *Chafetz Chaim* says that had our baseless hatred not been expressed openly in the form of *lashon hara,* the exile would long since have ended. We are still waiting for an answer to King Shaul's question: Why has the son of Yishai[1] not come, neither yesterday nor today, to the meal (אל הלחם)? The Munkaczer Rebbe locates the clue in the last words of the verse. He has not come because of strife (מלחמה)[2] and its outward manifestation, *lashon hara.*

◄ WHAT LASHON HARA DOES TO US

But if *lashon hara* has not ceased to be a problem for us, nei-

---

1. The son of Yishai was David, but the verse can also be read as refering to Mashiach, desendent of Yishai through David.
2. The root of מלחמה is לחם.

ther are we in the same position with respect to it that we were ten years ago. Then our principal efforts had to be directed at uprooting the most obvious types of *lashon hara*. We had no choice but to treat the symptoms, rather than the underlying causes of the disease, because the patient was hemorrhaging on the operating table. We are no longer in that situation today. As a community, we have matured and are now prepared to address some of the underlying causes of *lashon hara*.

By and large, the *lashon hara* that is still spoken today is far more subtle, less open, than one used to hear. It is the kind of *lashon hara* spoken between husband and wife or between best friends where the speaker is confident that whatever he or she says will go no further. It is not the kind of *lashon hara* that causes someone to be humiliated in the eyes of an entire community or to lose a job. So we might ask: What is so bad about this kind of speech? That is the first question I would like to address because until we realize the evil inherent in even this apparently harmless *lashon hara,* we will never be able to uproot it.

Let us look at the root of *lashon hara,* the first instance of destructive speech mentioned in the Torah. It did not take long for the Paradise that Hashem had created to be destroyed, and this started with the snake's speech to Chava. In trying to convince Chava to eat of the Tree of Knowledge, the snake tells her that the only reason that she has been forbidden to eat of it is that Hashem fears possible rivals. "Every artisan hates his rivals," the snake tells her, and Hashem is no different. He knows that if you eat of this tree, then you will be no different than He.

Hashem created the world for one and only one purpose: to bestow His *chesed* on mankind, and Gan Eden was the perfect expression of that desire. There angels literally waited on Adam *HaRishon* hand and foot. Adam did not have to work; he had nothing to do other than to experience his closeness to *Hakadosh Boruch Hu* and to enjoy all that Hashem had provided for him. Yet amidst all this good, this ultimate expression of Hashem's beneficence, the snake enters and sees evil. He accuses Hashem of petty jealousy.

That is the source of the evil: viewing life with a jaundiced eye, looking around oneself and seeing only the negative. The sin of the snake was exactly the same one repeated by the spies that Moshe sent to spy out the Land. To ensure their safety, *Hakadosh Baruch Hu* spread disease among those dwelling in the Land so that during the forty days the spies were in the Land, its inhabitants were occupied constantly in funerals and did not discover them. Instead of seeing in this the kindness of Hashem, however, the spies saw only the danger, and they reported that it is "a Land that consumes its inhabitants."

Lashon hara, no matter where it is spoken, then, involves taking a situation and focusing on the negative aspect. The person most directly hurt by doing so is the speaker himself, for in the process he makes himself into a negative person, the kind of person who finds the bad in any situation. When we train ourselves to find the bad and not the good, we destroy not only ourselves but everything and everyone around us. We become critical, negative people, and this affects our children, our spouses, all who come close to us. A child comes home with four A's and a B on his or her report card, and the only question is: Why the B? People who radiate such negativity can never have a satisfying marriage because whatever their spouses' merits, they see only the faults. And ultimately, such a person will show the same bitter attitude toward Hashem as well. He will always have complaints about the way *Hakadosh Baruch Hu* made the world or the life in which he finds himself.

In *Sha'arei Teshuvah* (III:217), *Rabbeinu Yonah* gives an

interesting interpretation of the verse (Mishlei 14:9): אוילים
יליץ אשם ובין ישרים רצון. Generally, this is understood to mean
that the fool, or sinner, needs something to intercede on his
behalf — whether a sacrifice or money — to propitiate those
against whom he has sinned. The upright, by contrast, enjoy
the good will of G-d and man. But *Rabbeinu Yonah* understood
the verse differently: "The fool pleads a fault" — i.e., he will
seek out another's failings and indict him — "but among the
upright there is good will" — i.e., they praise one in whom a
good thing is found. To illustrate the distinction, he cites the
case of a Torah sage and a certain person who passed the car-
cass of a rotting dog. The latter exclaimed over the putrid
smell; the Torah sage, however, noted, "How white are its
teeth." The fool only sees the negative; the wise man searches
out the positive in any situation.

Let me share with you a story from someone in our own time
who exemplified the attitude that *Rabbeinu Yonah* is describing. Rabbi Isser Zalman Meltzer was sitting in his *succah* during *Chol Hamoed*, and he asked Rabbi Dovid Finkel, who was
visiting him, to bring a pen and paper. Reb Dovid expressed
surprise that Reb Isser Zalman wanted to write on *Chol
Hamoed*, but Reb Isser Zalman told him that it was a matter of
pikuach nefesh (life or death). He then proceeded to write on
a piece of paper the verse (Mishlei 4:25): "עיניך לנכך יישרו
יביטו ועפעפיך — Let your eyes look opposite you, and your
eyelids look straight before you."

Reb Dovid was more than a little perplexed when he read
what Reb Isser Zalman had considered a matter of *pikuach
nefesh*. Reb Isser Zalman explained that during Succos hundreds of people would come to visit him — not all of them from
among the great scholars of Jerusalem. In their ranks would be
one or two mentally unbalanced people, with visible, and not
so visible, faults. Greeting and talking to such people, Reb
Isser Zalman wanted a constant reminder in front of him to
concentrate on their individual good points and those of every

Jew rather than on their faults. He remembered how the *Netziv* of Volozhin had explained the verse from *Mishlei:* "When you look at someone and discern a fault, turn your eyes inward and look at yourself instead."

Reb Isser Zalman's statement that this verse constituted *pikuach nefesh* for him was not just metaphorical. For metaphors one does not write on *Chol Hamoed*. Not focusing on the bad in people, things, and situations was, in his eyes, the key to not becoming a lonely, embittered person, lacking any joy in life.

✒ SO WHY DO WE DO IT?

A second step in attacking *lashon hara* at its roots is understanding the nature of the temptation. Why, if *lashon hara* is so bad for us, is it so hard for us to stop? Essentially *lashon hara* is a quick way of making us feel better about ourselves, a salve for fragile egos and poor self images. It helps us feel good about ourselves without any of the difficult work of actually striving to improve ourselves. Instead of raising ourselves, we lower others instead. When we put somebody else down, we feel instantly better. That is one of the reasons there is such a strong inclination to speak *lashon hara* about rabbis, *roshei yeshiva*, even *gedolei Yisrael*. If we can find fault with them, our sense of inferiority is lessened.

Plain, old-fashioned jealousy also plays a major role in much *lashon hara*. If we cannot have someone else's wealth or position, let us at least find something wrong with them. That is why there is so much danger of *lashon hara* within families. Some of it goes back to sibling rivalry and feelings that a brother or sister was favored over us.

In today's information age, knowledge about things that are not generally known — who is getting divorced or going bankrupt, what prospective match broke up — is power. Being the first to reveal something is thus a cheap ego trip. It should be noted, however, that it is not only cheap but brief, for as soon as one reveals the juicy little tidbit, the power of knowing what others do not is gone.

In sum, the temptations of lashon hara are greatest the weaker our self-image, the more insecure we are. And we should ask ourselves if that is the way we want to see ourselves, or the kind of people we want to be.

☙ LEARNING TO LOVE YOUR FELLOW JEW

As we all know it was Rabbi Akiva who identified "Love your brother as yourself" as the great principle of the Torah. Therefore if we want to understand how to reach this level, we would do well to study his character. One can find throughout the Talmud numerous examples where everyone else could only find the bad in a certain situation and Rabbi Akiva showed them the same situation from a different perspective. The most famous, of course, is the Gemara at the very end of Makkos. Rabbi Akiva was walking with his colleagues, and they come to Har HaBayis (the Temple Mount) and saw a fox coming out of the ruins of the Kodesh Kodoshim (Holy of Holies). They cried and he rejoiced. They cried to find foxes frolicking in a place so holy that a non-Kohen was subject to the death penalty for entering. Rabbi Akiva, however, pointed out to them that the prophet Yeshaya linked together Uriah HaKohen and Zechariah in his prophecy even though one lived in the time of the First Temple and the other in the time of the Second Temple. "I am rejoicing," Rabbi Akiva explained, "because now that I have seen the prophecy of Uriah fulfilled — 'Zion shall be ploughed over like a field' (Micha 3:12) — I know that so too will the prophecy of Zechariah be fulfilled — 'Old men and women will again dwell in the streets of Jerusalem' (*Zechariah* 8:5)."

Rabbi Akiva had himself lived in the time of the *Bais Hamikdash* and witnessed its destruction, and the Jews of his time still lived with the memory of the *Bais Hamikdash* etched strongly in their memories. On Yom Kippur, they were despondent over what was no longer: e.g., the service of the *Kohen Gadol* and the crimson thread that turned white to show that *Klal Yisrael* had been purified of its sins with the sending of the *Seir HaMishtaleach* (Scapegoat) to Azazel. Again it was Rabbi Akiva who consoled them. He told them to celebrate the fact that they now had a direct route to Hashem with no intermediaries: "Happy are you, Israel! Before whom are you purified and Who purifies you. Your Father in Heaven."

The same ability that Rabbi Akiva had to find the bright side of every situation was what allowed him to see the Divine spark in every fellow Jew and to love them as himself. He ignored the foibles and faults and concentrated on the essence. That is what we do with ourselves, and it is what we are commanded to do with respect to our fellow Jews as well. Thus the *Ba'al Shem Tov* explained the concept of loving your friend as yourself:

> Are you perfect or do you have faults? And when you notice those faults, what do you say? That's not the real me. I'm basically a good person who happens to have a few faults. That is how you are commanded to view your fellow Jew as well.

Once again Rabbi Isser Zalman Meltzer is an exemplar of this ability to see the Divine image in our fellow Jews. Someone once told Reb Isser Zalman that the Brisker Rav was on his way to visit him. Reb Isser Zalman rushed to put on his Shabbos clothes and to set the table in a manner appropriate to receive the Brisker Rav. In the end, it turned out that Reb Isser Zalman's informant had erred. He had seen a simple Jew who happened to look like the Brisker Rav. Reb Isser Zalman nevertheless rushed out to bring the Jew into his home, and proceeded to wait on him as if he would have been the Brisker Rav. Later Reb Isser Zalman explained his behavior: "The truth is we have to treat every Jew like the Brisker Rav. But our lack of time and patience prevents us from doing so. If, however, the *Ribbono shel Olam* furnished me with this opportunity to treat a Jew as he should be treated, I did not want to lose it."

If we learn to view our fellow Jews in this light and to treat them accordingly, we will spare ourselves a tremendous amount of anguish not only in this world but also in the next. The *Reishis Chochmah* cites a truly frightening *Chazal* which states that at the moment of death a person sees the *Malach HaMaves,* the Angel of Death. His head is full of eyes and his sword is drawn. The Angel of Death asks us four questions, and depending on how we answer them, our death will either be serene or terrifying. (These four questions are aside from those asked later in Heaven.) Those questions are: Did you learn Torah or aid your husband in learning Torah? Did you do acts of kindness? Did you recite *Krias Shema* morning and evening? And finally, did you treat your fellow Jew as a king?

What does it mean to treat your fellow Jew as a king? It means discovering the strengths and assets of our fellow Jew and making them stand out in our mind. Our entire transition to the next world is contingent on how well we succeed.

➷ PUTTING OUR NEW ATTITUDE INTO PRACTICE

The *Sefer HaChinuch* tells us that a person's external actions have the power to transform his inner being as well. Thus if we want to start viewing our fellow Jews in a more positive light, the starting point is treating them differently. Begin with the little things: not slamming the horn if the driver in front of you is not halfway through the light by the time it turns green, giving someone a chance to parallel park without honking. Next we can start wishing people we see on the street and in *shul* a good Shabbos even if we have not known them since kindergarten. We can invite those new to the community, who often feel forlorn and forsaken, for a Shabbos meal. And when we talk to one another, let us put aside the mental calculators that make our minds whirr like a computer as we add up the cost of our friend's *sheitel,* dress, and shoes.

The *Shem MiShmuel* writes that loving our fellow Jew like ourselves is something which we are capable of because at some level our fellow Jews are, in fact, part of ourselves. We all come from the same soul root, and therefore the deeper we go into our spiritual essence the more we find identity. The degree to which we find ourselves bound to our fellow Jews is a reflection of our own spiritual level. The more we focus on externals — e.g., the more we reduce each of our fellow Jews to the type of head-covering he wears — the more we will see only differences and division; the more we become people of spirit, the deeper will be our focus on spiritual qualities. And at that level we will find unity and identity. The ability to find the *pintele Yid* (essential core of Jewishness) in our fellow Jew is therefore the measure of our own spiritual status.

We began with the Gulf War and we will end there as well. For the six weeks of the war, from January 15 to February 28, we all felt the threat to *Eretz Yisrael,* and out of the shared feeling that our most precious possession was in danger we came together as *Klal Yisrael.* We came together, and Hashem responded with open miracles. For six weeks we were on a qualitatively higher level, we were a community, and the results were obvious to all. In a sense, we relived the exodus from Egypt. For there too the miracles came in response to an internal unity among us. The *Ohr Somayach* writes that even though the Jews in Egypt worshiped idols and did not keep *bris milah,* nevertheless they did not speak *lashon hara* and they loved one another, and for that they merited all the miracles that Hashem did for them.

On the verse, "And He was king in Yeshurun, when the heads of the people and the tribes of Israel were gathered together" (Devarim 33:5), the *Sifri* comments: When will the *Ribbono shel Olam* again be King in Yeshurun? When the tribes of Israel are again unified and not divided into various little subgroups and cliques. Then will we witness the greatest miracle of all: the ingathering of all the Jews of the world from their lands of dispersion to Jerusalem.

Humility Versus Self-Esteem

One of the difficulties of addressing this topic is that so many of the terms of the discussion are borrowed from contemporary psychology, and it is therefore frequently hard to know where the Torah viewpoint ends and modern psychology begins. Let us just take one such term: self-esteem.

American education for the last 20 years has placed the student's self-esteem at the very top of the educational agenda.

As a consequence, American students consistently rank high-est of those of all developed nations in their self-evaluation of their educational attainments. Unfortunately, they have at the same time the least cause to think so well of themselves: By all standardized measures, they rank well below their contempo-raries in other developed countries. Here, clearly, is an instance of the pursuit of self-esteem gone haywire, for it is self-esteem not based on a solid base of real life achievement.

At the same time, we shall see that an absence of a positive self-image can prevent us from being the type of Jews that we could and should be.

Mishlei refers to a haughty heart as an abomination to G-d. The term abomination is a particularly strong one indi-cating a personality flaw so great that it affects every single aspect of a person's being. Given how despicable this quality is in the eyes of the Torah, we have to ask ourselves whether we are not fostering a negative *middah* when we praise our children. Are we turning them into conceited people? Is an appreciation of one's talents and gifts the same as being a *ba'al ga'avah* despised by Hashem? These are just a few of the questions we will be addressing.

◆ ON BECOMING A NOTHING

One of the famous European schools of *mussar* taught its adherents to constantly work on achieving a feeling of worth-lessness, of being a nothing. There is at least one sense from a Torah point of view — and I would submit only one — in which we must view ourselves as nothings: in relation to *Hakadosh Boruch Hu.*

In *Hilchos Yesodei HaTorah,* the *Rambam* discusses the mitzvos of both loving and fearing Hashem and how one goes about attaining the love and fear of Hashem. Through the contemplation of the wonders of Creation, writes the *Rambam,* will one come to the Love of G-d. When we consider the magnitude of the universe, the symmetry of nature, the way every aspect of the human body fulfills a specific function while each is coordinated with the others, we are overwhelmed by Hashem's greatness and the good He has bestowed on His creation. And when one considers his place in the cosmos, says the *Rambam,* he will immediately draw back in fright and recognize himself as a tiny, insignificant speck in the universe.

If you have never experienced G-d as an overwhelming presence, go to the Grand Canyon. Viewing the Grand Canyon was one of my lifelong ambitions, and a few summers ago, thanks to frequent flyer miles, my wife and I had the opportunity to do so. We entered Grand Canyon National Park towards evening. At the first overlook, Mather's Point, there was only one thought coursing through my mind: Who but G-d created this? Looking out over the miles and miles of majestic cliffs overhanging the canyon, there is, in fact, a powerful feeling of G-d's presence. At the same time, one feels his insignificance in His grand scheme. It was one of the most religious experiences of my life.

Nor am I alone in this feeling. A *ba'alas teshuvah* once approached me after a lecture and told me that her journey back began not at the *Kosel,* nor in *Eretz Yisrael,* nor at someone's Shabbos table, but at the Grand Canyon. Another woman once asked me if I had noticed that everyone whispers at the Grand Canyon. There is a sense of awe and trembling that comes with the feeling of standing in the presence of the Creator that makes normal human discourse seem out of place. That's the feeling, by the way, we should have in *shul* during *davening* but usually do not, unfortunately.

A person who achieves this awareness of his own insignificance and powerlessness in comparison to Hashem can never be a *ba'al ga'avah* (arrogant person). That is why, writes the Telzer *Rav* Rabbi Yosef Leib Bloch, Moshe *Rabbeinu* was the most humble of all men. Because he lived in the most intimate proximity to Hashem of any human being who ever lived, he also had the greatest awareness of the absolute chasm between a created being and the Creator. Our problems with arrogance derive from our lack of the same constant awareness of Hashem's presence.

✒ HUMILITY OR STUPIDITY?

Humility, in the Jewish view, does not mean a lack of awareness of one's talents. If one is intelligent, humility does not consist of thinking of oneself as stupid. If one is handsome, it does not consist in thinking oneself ugly. That, Rabbi Leib Chasman once said, is not humility; it is stupidity. At the same time, it does not hurt to keep in mind that everything is relative, and that being the "best boy" in *shiur* does not make one the Vilna Gaon or Reb Chaim Brisker.

Even an awareness of one's spiritual attainments — as opposed to his G-d-given gifts and talents — is not inconsistent with the highest degree of humility. When Nadav and Avihu were killed by a Divine fire on the day of the dedication of the Tabernacle, Moshe *Rabbeinu* told their father Aharon that he had known long in advance that something of this nature would occur, for Hashem had said that He would be sanctified through His close ones. "I knew that the Tabernacle would be sanctified through someone in whom G-d's glory reposes," Moshe told Aharon, " but I thought it would be you or me."

In other words, Moshe assumed that he and Aharon, as the two holiest members of *Klal Yisrael,* would be the sacrifices. Moshe knew that it was he to whom G-d had chosen to give His Torah; he knew that there would never be another prophet like him; and he knew he was the teacher of *Klal Yisrael* throughout all the generations. Being the humblest of men, then, is not inconsistent with knowing oneself to be the holiest of men.

The London Beis Din, of which Rabbi Yechezkel Abramsky was the head, once had to fire a certain *shochet,* who promptly sued the *Beis Din* in civil court. Rabbi Abramsky was called to testify, and one of the questions concerned his qualifications as a halachic expert. He was asked if he was the United Kingdom's leading halachic authority. Rabbi Abramsky answered in the affirmative. At that point, the judge interjected and asked Rabbi Abramsky whether such a statement was not inconsistent with the Jewish emphasis on humility. "Your honor," Rabbi Abramsky replied, "I am under oath."

Humility did not require Rabbi Abramsky to ignore what was universally acknowledged, i.e., that he was one of the greatest living Torah scholars and certainly the preeminent one in Great Britain in his day. Humility required him to be grateful for the prodigious natural gifts with which he was favored. Even with respect to his phenomenal self-sacrifice — much of his classic 20-volume commentary on *Tosefta, Chazon Yechezkel,* was written in a Soviet labor camp with no *seforim* available — humility required that he acknowledge "for that were you created." But it did not require him to deny the facts.

✎ HINTS ON HUMILITY

An awareness of one's talents is, as we have seen, not inconsistent with humility. Nevertheless, that awareness can lead to an unattractive conceitedness. To avoid that it is worth keeping in mind that natural gifts in particular reflect no merit on their possessor. If you were born intelligent, if you were born good looking, if you were born well to do, these circumstances of birth all have one thing in common: You did nothing to deserve any of it. You have been the recipient of a completely unearned gift from Hashem. And the same is true of all inherited abilities or wealth.

Even the term gift applied to the bounty that Hashem showers upon us is too strong a term. It is, in fact, a loan, something that can be reclaimed by the true owner at any moment. The *Mishnah* at the end of *Sotah* (49a) states that with the death of *Rabbeinu HaKadosh,* Rebbi Yehudah HaNasi, true *anavah,* humility, disappeared from the world. In a very enigmatic comment, the *Amora* Rav Yosef challenges the statement of the *Mishnah,* and says, "There is still me." At first glance, Rav Yosef seems to be bragging about what a humble person he is. Inasmuch as *Amoraim* are not generally given to jokes or to challenging the conclusions of a *Mishnah* unless they have a Tannaitic source of their own that contradicts it, Rav Yosef's statement cries out for elaboration.

To understand what Rav Yosef meant it is necessary to know something of his personal history. One of the greatest of the *Amoraim,* mentioned numerous times throughout *Shas,* he went blind in the middle of his life. With blindness came something far worse: Rav Yosef forgot all his learning. Many times his students had to remind him of things that he had previously taught them. Rav Yosef, then, was an object lesson in the transitory nature of all that one has in this world. Whether it be wealth, success, physical beauty, children, or even Torah learning, everything, G-d forbid, can be lost. And that is what Rav Yosef was saying: The *Mishnah* teaches that there is no more humility in the world after Rebbi. That is not so. If people have to learn humility, let them reflect on what happened to me and consider how impermanent is all that upon which they pride themselves.

With recognition that everything we have is a gift from Hashem — and a provisional one at that — goes a tremendous responsibility. If we have been favored by G-d with certain talents through no merit of our own, it can only be because He wants us to use those talents in a particular way. Thus the greater the ability the greater the responsibility. Recognizing this, the gifts we have been given are simply a trust from

Hashem rather than an occasion for pride. Moshe was the most gifted person who ever lived — at birth he already emitted a light of holiness that filled the room. Yet far from being a contradiction to his humility, those gifts were the source of it. Moshe's humility consisted in the way his talents were consecrated completely to Hashem's purposes.

Natural gifts or success in life, then, do not necessarily make a person into a *ba'al ga'avah.* Quite the contrary, when they are understood as something given provisionally for Hashem's purposes, they cause their possessor to turn his focus from himself to the Creator and His desires.

THE BA'AL GA'AVAH

We might ask what exactly is so terrible about someone we refer to as a *ba'al ga'avah,* someone who takes great pride in his abilities. With some negative *middos* — anger, stinginess, dishonesty, for example — it is obvious that these traits make a person very hard to live with. But why should it bother me if someone thinks he is G-d's gift to humanity? Regardless of whether his evaluation of his natural gifts is accurate or not, his conceit would seem to be a matter of grave indifference.

The answer as to why the *ba'al ga'avah* is both repugnant to others and an abomination to Hashem lies in his or her self-absorption. Having failed to acknowledge that talents are undeserved gifts or to recognize that with those gifts attaches responsibility, the *ba'al ga'avah* views them only as means of self-aggrandizement.

A Jew is by definition a member of a community, part of *Klal Yisrael.* The *ba'al ga'avah,* however, is unsuited to communal life, unable to view himself as one limb of a collective body striving for a common purpose. He sees the world only in terms of "I" and "me."

The tale of someone who becomes rich and rejects all his old friends as somehow beneath him is already commonplace. Rebbe Yechiel Michel of Zelotshov had such a *chassid*. One day the man came to visit Reb Yechiel Michel, and the latter took him to a window and asked him what he saw. The *chassid* replied that he saw people going about their daily affairs. Then Reb Yechiel Michel took him to a mirror and asked him what he saw. "Myself," replied the *chassid*.

"Know," said Reb Yechiel Michel, "that the only difference between a window and a mirror is a little bit of silver covering the glass." The little silver in his pocket, Reb Yechiel Michel was telling his *chassid,* had transformed him from someone capable of seeing others to one capable only of seeing himself. So it is with all forms of pride and conceit.

To one degree or another most of us suffer from egocentricity, a tendency to view the whole world only in relation to ourselves. Who has not had the experience of greeting someone he knows well and receiving an unexpectedly curt reply? Afterwards we spend hours wracking our brains to figure out how we could have offended this friend. Those hours are a form of egocentricity. Why should we think someone else's bad mood has anything to do with us, as if we were the cause of everyone else's ups and downs? Why do we ignore all the more probable explanations — money pressures, a headache, concerns over a child — for an explanatory scheme that puts us at the center of the action?

A wise man once said that until the age of 20 a person spends all his time worrying about what others think of him; from 20 to 40, he adopts an attitude of being oblivious to what others think; only at 40 does he realize that others are not in fact thinking about him at all. The trouble is that many of us never reach stage three; we remain convinced that everyone else's thoughts center on us.

The world is full of people who talk and act as if they have a very high opinion of themselves. But the truth is that a real honest-to-goodness *ba'al ga'avah* is hard, if not impossible, to find. If one scratches the surface of the run-of-the mill conceited person, one inevitably finds a mass of insecurities. The image of superiority which the *ba'al ga'avah* attempts to project becomes for them a prison.

Such a person cannot accept criticism because to do so is to admit that one has faults, and for a fragile ego that is too much to admit. Such a person cannot say "I'm sorry" because doing so requires an admission of having been wrong. Such a person is reluctant to try new things or undertake projects in which he might fail because failure is too threatening for him.

The *ba'al ga'avah* acts haughty, looks haughty, talks haughty, but underneath it all he is a very scared human being whose life revolves around protecting an image in which he himself does not believe.

From this follows a surprising conclusion: Recognition of one's abilities is not inconsistent with *anavah,* as we demonstrated above. Furthermore, a healthy self-image is a necessary condition for being able to act modestly and for virtually every other good trait as well. A person without a healthy self-image spends his entire time shoring up his fragile image, and has no time to think about others or his relationship to them, except as it affects his view of himself.

A person who feels good about himself is capable of accepting and even using criticism from his superiors. He does not assume criticism is an attack on him, but views it as a useful means of improving himself. A person who feels good about himself does not have to dominate and terrorize subordinates because he does not have to see others quiver in front of him to feel secure. A person who feels good about himself is not afraid to apologize to his wife or children. The irony, then, is that a positive self-image allows one to act with humility.

BUILDING A POSITIVE SELF-IMAGE

Once we realize the importance of a positive self-image, the next question is: How do we instill such a self-image in our children so that they can reach their full potential and are capable of establishing deep relationships with others, which are not just battlegrounds for proving oneself?

To answer that question, let me share the following parable. A tourist was once sailing from one South Sea island to another. Before he came to one particular island, the tour guide told him that on this island lived one of the most remarkable natural businessmen in the world. This native was known never to have been bested in any negotiation, and had acquired fabulous wealth by the standards of the islands, including the only eight-cow wife on the island. Noticing the quizzical look on the tourist's face, the guide explained that the average wife was purchased for one or two cows. Even a girl with every desirable quality could not expect to fetch more than four cows, and a purchase price of more than five or six cows was unheard of. Yet this man had an eight-cow wife.

They landed on the island, and the guide took the tourist to meet this extraordinary businessman. As they sat talking in his tent, the businessman asked the tourist whether he would like his wife to bring them some refreshments. By this time, the tourist's curiosity had gotten the better of him, and he replied affirmatively. Shortly thereafter, the local tycoon's wife entered. His guest saw a graceful, modest woman obviously eager to please her husband. He had no doubt that she was a fine wife for a South Sea islander, but was a little perplexed as to what had distinguished her to such an extent. After the wife had returned to the tent, the native turned to his guest and said, "You've probably heard that I'm a shrewd businessman, who drives a hard bargain. You probably heard as well that I paid the extraordinary sum of eight cows for my wife, and you are wondering why.

"When I met my wife, she looked nothing like she does today. She slouched and generally carried herself poorly. But for whatever reason, I decided she was the girl I wanted to marry. I asked myself what I could do to give her more presence, more confidence. In the end, I realized that the key was making her feel that I viewed her as the most special woman on the island. So that is why I paid a price unheard of in the history of the island. And I was right. Overnight the knowledge of how highly I valued her transformed her into the wonderful woman you see today."

Here is a similar story from a much holier source. A young woman once came to the *Chazon Ish* to discuss a match. The *Chazon Ish* made every effort to find out what was causing the girl to hesitate. Finally, she blurted out that the young man in question just did not carry himself like her father did. Her image of what a husband should be was her father, and this young man did not seem to have the requisite confidence. The *Chazon Ish* told her that if she treated him just as her mother treated her father, he would become the husband she imagined. If she showed him the same respect, he would, in turn, show the same confidence in himself.

We all know the famous story of how Rachel, the daughter of Kalba Savua, married an ignorant shepherd named Akiva and sent him off to learn shortly after their marriage. When he first returned home after 12 years, Rabbi Akiva arrived at the door of his hut poised to knock. There he overheard a neighbor berating him to his wife for his callousness in having abandoned her for 12 years. Rachel told her neighbor that she would rejoice if he spent another 12 years learning Torah. Rabbi Akiva immediately turned and went back to his studies without even greeting his wife. Twelve years later, he returned home again, this time accompanied by 24,000 students. His wife rushed to greet him but none of the *talmidim* knew who she was, and they refused to let her pass. Rabbi Akiva ordered them to let her through with those immortal words, "All that is mine and all that is yours is hers."

Simply understood, Rabbi Akiva meant that she had the merit of his Torah for having let him study without interruption for 24 years. But there is a deeper meaning to those words. Rabbi Akiva was saying, "I was an *am ha'aretz,* a complete ignoramus, and only because she believed in me and saw potential I did not even know I had was I able to become Rabbi Akiva the Tanna, Rabbi Akiva the teacher of 24,000 disciples. Her confidence in me was what made me. Without her, I would have remained an ignorant shepherd all my life."

The greatest gift we can give our children is faith in themselves. After I spoke on this topic in one city, a woman approached me and told me how she had a retarded child who had more self-confidence than all her other children. At three months, this child had suddenly stopped growing or developing in any way. The experts told this woman and her husband that they should institutionalize the child because he would never walk or talk. But this woman refused to accept that. For the next four years, she devoted herself exclusively to this child. Today, he learns *Chumash,* plays ball, goes to school. And though he will never be the brightest boy in his class, he feels great about himself.

I told this woman that she should have given the lecture, not me, and asked her how she and her husband had instilled such self-confidence in their son. She answered:

> *Every step of the way, every accomplishment, we made a big deal about. When he first put together three words, we made a kiddush; when he learned his first posuk of*

Chumash, we made a siyum. We weren't embarrassed; we were proud of him. We made him believe in himself and what he could accomplish on his level.

If we can instill that same belief in our children — and even before that in ourselves — we and they can be truly humble people who know that Hashem has created us with unique talents for a task that only we can perform. Armed with that knowledge, we will be capable of fulfilling the tasks for which He created us.

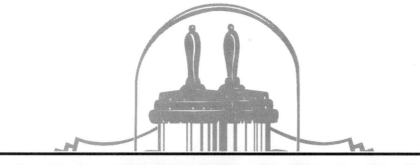

CONTEMPORARY
ISSUES

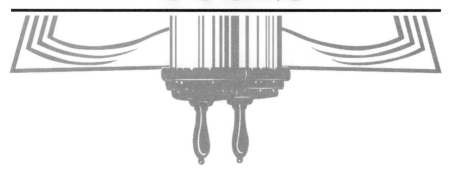

The Jewish Family
in a Changing World

I hope I will not be suspected of being an aspiring presidential candidate for addressing the subject of Family Values. I am not. In the immortal words of General William Tecumseh Sherman, "If nominated, I will not run; if elected, I will not serve."

As we survey American Orthodoxy at century's end, there is indeed much of which we can be proud. We have witnessed a veritable renaissance of Orthodox Jewish life. The vibrancy and vitality of American Orthodox life today could scarcely have been imagined 50 years ago. This is so not just in major Jewish centers like New York, Baltimore, and Chicago, but in dozens of smaller communities as well.

I have been privileged to witness this phenomena personally the last several years when my family and I returned to my hometown of Seattle to spend Pesach with my mother, may she live and be well. When I was growing up in Seattle in the '50s, there were 150 to 200 Jews in *shul* for *davening* on the first day of *Yom Tov*, but at *Minchah* only 25 or so Jews returned for *davening*. Today almost all will be back for *Minchah*. As a child, I remember that there was an overflow crowd on the eighth day of Pesach of those who came for *Yizkor.* Today there is not much difference between the eighth day and the rest of the *Yom Tov* — just Jews who come to *shul* because a Jew goes to *shul* every day.

But before we start congratulating ourselves on all that has been achieved, I must tell you that not all is well with us. We are still in *galus* (exile), and for all that America has been, and continues to be, a *malchus shel chesed* (a kingdom of kindness) for the Jew, it is still *galus*. And this exile is taking its toll on us.

We all know the famous *Rashi* at the beginning of *Vayishlach* on Yaakov's message to Esav, ". . . with Lavan I dwelled (גרתי)" (Bereishis 32:5). The *gematria* of גרתי is 613, and *Rashi* explains Yaakov's subtle message as: Even though I dwelt with Lavan, I kept all 613 mitzvos and did not learn from his evil ways. My Rosh Yeshiva, Rav Ruderman *zt"l*, once asked: "Isn't this *Rashi* redundant? If Yaakov kept all 613 mitzvos, is it not obvious that he did not adopt the ways of Lavan? Doesn't the statement 'I kept all the mitzvos' encompass not having followed in Lavan's ways?"

The answer, *Rashi* teaches us, is: We can have Dial-a-Daf and Dial-a-Shiur, and *cholov Yisrael,* and kosher pizza, and kosher Chinese food, and still not be free of the influence of the nations in which we dwell. I do not think any of us can say that we have not emulated the values and lifestyles of America, that in everything we do our only guideline has been the Torah.

Historically Jews have always taken on certain traits of their host country. It is no accident, for instance, that German Jews are renowned for their punctuality. They were punctual because Germans are punctual. And if it is true that we are inevitably influenced by our host culture, we have to ask ourselves precisely what is the nature of American society as we approach the end of the century.

Let us start with the least dangerous aspect of our contemporary culture. Today's America is a society caught up with triviality. Life for a Jew is meant to be an earnest endeavor. Every moment of our lives, we are either approaching closer to Hashem or removing ourselves from Him. There is no moment not imbued with tremendous potential to fulfill the Divine Will.

This sense of seriousness is not reinforced, to put it mildly, by contemporary society. Is there anyone who has not heard the coffee commercial: "The best part of waking up is Folger's in your cup." When I was in yeshiva, the wake-up call was: "Arise to the service of your Creator." Today, however, we are told that the best part of waking up is to have the sponsor's brand of coffee.

We live in a country that earnestly debated the question of whether an upcoming memorial postage stamp should show an entertainer in his youth or in his bloated, drug-addicted middle age. It would be nice if any issue of truly national significance received as much attention from our electorate. When Crayola Crayon Company decided to remove raw umber and maize from its box of 64 colors, over 300 people a day wrote in to protest this break with tradition. A society, the Raw Umber Preservation Society of America, was even formed to protest the change.

We live in a sports-crazed society. One hundred and twenty million people watch the Super Bowl, but only 90 million the State of the Union Address. And do not think this has not reached us. There is a noticeable decline in Torah lectures on January Sundays because that is the NFL play-off season.

Closely related to the triviality of American society is its tolerance. Both are a result of a lack of any sense of ultimate values. Because nothing is viewed, in the end, as of any importance, there is nothing wrong with spending time on trivialities. At the same time, there is no reason to fight with my neighbor over anything since our differences are nothing more than matters of personal opinion.

In truth, it is a blessing for us that America is such a tolerant society. If it were not, they would not tolerate us either. But as Jews there are ways in which we dare not adopt this "live and let live" attitude. By that I do not mean, of course, the intolerance of every minute difference within the Orthodox world. That is destructive of our fundamental unity. What I mean is a certain apathy about the children next door who intermarry and the neighbor across the street who mows his lawn every Shabbos. A lack of concern that most Jewish children in the Western world can name the mother of Yeshu but few can name the mother of Moses; a lack of concern that they know the words to Silent Night but not *Maoz Tzur*. It is important for our non-religious neighbors to know how deeply we care about these things. Just showing our concern can sometimes be our most powerful weapon.

I recently met a *ba'al teshuvah* couple in Atlanta, and they told me how they became religious. When they were first married, they lived in an apartment complex, and every Saturday morning was laundry day. One Shabbos as the wife was carrying the laundry to the washing machines an older Jewish widow stopped her and asked, "How can you do your laundry today?

It's Shabbos!" The younger woman explained that Saturday was her only free day, but the widow was undeterred. Week after week, she would stop the younger woman and tell her the same thing, "But it's Shabbos." She said this without anger or venom, just pain. And there was certainly nothing philosophical or deep about what she said. But when that couple started to become religious, it is no accident that the first change they made in their life was finding another laundry day.

Today's America is, let us face it, a dangerous place. Take the schools, for instance. In the 1940s a survey was taken of public school teachers concerning their most severe discipline problems. They were: talking in class, chewing gum in school, running in the halls, jumping out of turn in line, and not putting paper into the wastepaper basket. A similar survey 40 years later listed the following major problems: drug abuse, lethal weapons in schools, pregnancy, suicide, assault, and robbery. Those two surveys provide a fair measure of the direction in which our society is moving.

So while I would be the first to admit that the yeshiva education that my children are receiving today is superior to my day school education in Seattle 40 years ago, at the same time the general environment in which my children are growing up is far more detrimental, one far more inimical to Jewish values. In terms of basic *derech eretz,* I am not even sure if the public schools of my youth were not superior to many religious schools today.

NO SHAME

The single most damaging aspect of contemporary American society, however, is not its trivial pursuits or its "live and let live" tolerance; it is the total loss of the sense of shame. It is a society in which you can pretty much do what you want, say what you want, sing what you want, and wear what you want. When Vice President Dan Quayle suggested that there might be something worrisome about the glorification of unwed motherhood, and its treatment as a comic subject, he found himself subjected to endless ridicule. Compare this to the attitude toward this subject just 20 years ago, and you derive a sense of where we are headed.

Three characteristics distinguish the Jewish people: their compassion, their sense of shame, and their generosity (*Yevamos* 79). Each of these three characteristics is a legacy from one of the *Avos*. We are *gomlei chasadim* (doers of kindness) because Avraham *Avinu* instilled that trait in us. We are compassionate because Yaakov *Avinu* was compassionate. And our profound sense of shame is a legacy from Yitzchak *Avinu*.

We know that the defining characteristic of Yitzchak *Avinu* was his fear of G-d, and that trait is inextricably intertwined with the sense of shame. Fear of G-d is above all a reflection of standing at every moment in the presence of an infinitely greater Being before Whom one is utterly ashamed. Thus the *Rema* begins his commentary to the codification of Jewish law with the words, "Place Hashem opposite you at all times."

Without shame there can be no *teshuvah* (repentance) either. *Rebbe* said, "עז פנים לגהינום — A brazen person goes to *Gehinnom*." He was asked, "What if he repents?" to which he replied, "He cannot do *teshuvah*." Repentance is beyond someone who is sure that he is always right and never experiences the feeling of having to submit before a Being infinitely greater than himself.

The *Maharal* writes that a society without shame or inhibition will be permeated with brazenness and *chutzpah*. It will be a society devoid of respect for elders or for authority of any kind. The *Maharal* continues — and remember that these words were written more than 300 years ago — such a society will be characterized by moral bankruptcy and rampant promiscuity. Was he predicting the society recently described by the Chaplain of the United States Senate?

> *We demand freedom without restraint, rights without responsibility, choice without consequences, pleasure without pain. In our narcissistic, hedonistic, masochistic, valueless preoccupation, we are becoming a people dominated by lust, avarice and greed.*

We must not — dare not — convince ourselves that we remain unaffected by these trends around us. We do not. We can point to our hundreds of *Daf Yomi shiurim* and to our children's study of Mishnah by heart, and the fact that they are learning ten times as much as we did at their age. But we are not entitled to any assumption that we have thereby sealed ourselves off from the surrounding society.

I was in a major department store recently, and in front of me was a mother wheeling around a cart into which she was putting hundreds of dollars worth of clothes for the little darling who was accompanying her. The latter was speaking to her the whole time as if he were doing her the greatest imaginable favor in allowing her to shower him with expensive gifts. Hopefully, our children do not talk exactly like this, but the influence seeps in. Principals and teachers in our schools complain constantly that there is a lack of *derech eretz*. Children regard themselves as great wits, with a full assortment of one-liners for the entertainment of their classmates.

Not so many generations ago, several generations were likely to occupy the same house — children were likely to live with their grandparents as well as their parents. And as a consequence, children saw their parents showing respect and deference to their grandparents. They had in front of them models of *kibud av v'eim*. Our children, by contrast, rarely have a chance to see us accepting authority. They rarely see us together with our parents. Nor do they see us accepting the authority of our *rabbonim*. How often do they hear, "We can't do this because the *rav* said not to." Because they do not see us displaying respect for authority they have fewer models from which to learn it.

Let us not fool ourselves. We also have in many of our communities major problems with the *tznius* of women's dress, which is perhaps the greatest manifestation of a lack of shame. Nothing else can explain certain modes of attire — often with husbands' explicit or complicit encouragement — other than a loss of *bushah* (shame). The hems and sleeves may technically be of the prescribed length, and yet everything about the garment is contrary to the spirit of *tznius*.

Dayan Aaron Dovid Dunner of London relates how Rabbi Moshe Feinstein was once asked whether certain styles conformed to the requirements of *tznius*. He replied that they did not. But when he was requested to put his *psak* in writing, he refused. Pressed for an explanation of his reluctance, he said, sadly, "What the designers say in Paris has more weight than my *psak halachah*."

As a people we are commanded to be *kedoshim* (holy beings). *Rashi* interprets the word *kadosh,* holy, to refer to separation and abstention from the pleasures around us. Overindulgence in the pleasures of the material world, conspicuous consumption, will, we are taught, make us vulgar. We will lose the spiritual elevation, the *kedushah,* that is meant to be our defining characteristic. And that is happening to us. We tend to think of restraint and abstinence as the exclusive province of a few holy men in Bnei Brak and Jerusalem — and certainly not as something that should worry us overly much in our choice of cars, in our vacations, in our homes and the way they are furnished. But to be holy — קדושים תהיו— is a

Divine injunction to each of us to avoid the morass of consumerism, self-indulgence and instant gratification that define so much of modern American life.

When we fail to do that, the consequences are frightening. We are commanded to be holy so that He Who is holy can dwell in our midst offering His protective shield: "Your encampment must be holy because Hashem walks in the midst of your encampment to save you" (Devarim 23:15). And when we lose our sense of shame, and with it the ability to stand apart as a holy people, then Hashem can no longer find his place in our midst and we are left without His protection. Without that protection, we experience *hester panim* (hiding of the Divine countenance) — terrible accidents, young children dying, mothers and fathers of large families struck by cancer and heart attacks in the prime of life, *rachmona l'tzlan.*

☙ INTO OUR SEALED ROOMS

So what can we do? First, we can follow the advice of the prophet, "Then those who fear Hashem spoke one to the other" (Malachi 3:16). Just focusing on the problem and sensitizing ourselves to it is the first step. *Shiurim* and lectures that increase the level of awareness of those areas that restore holiness to our lives — *tznius, taharas hamishpachah, mikveh* — are one step.

During the Gulf War, a term that became very familiar to all of us as we worried about our Jewish brothers in *Eretz Yisrael* was the "sealed room," the room in which Israeli families took refuge as Saddam Hussein directed his SCUD missiles towards *Eretz Yisrael.* The great fear was that those SCUDs would be armed with poison gas, and so families rushed to rooms as hermetically sealed as possible and put on their gas masks.

What I have been trying to describe is a poisonous atmosphere that surrounds us and that requires us to create our own sealed rooms. Let me give you an example of one person who took this imperative to protect himself and his family very seriously. (I am not offering the example of what he did as necessarily one to emulate, but rather as an indication of the type of sensitivity that it is incumbent upon us to develop.)

This person was on an airplane flight with his whole family when the in-flight movie came on. No one in his family took headsets, but as the movie progressed, he saw that the visual images on screen were precisely the type from which he had been trying to shield his family for twenty years. He immediately rang the flight attendant and said that he wanted to complain to the pilot. The stewardess, needless to say, told him that he could not speak to the pilot and that the show must go on, whatever his personal tastes.

The gentleman in question — who was, by the way, an imposing fellow, at least 6'5" tall — did not take this passively. He simply went up to the movie screen and pushed it right back up into the ceiling. With that, the pilot suddenly materialized. The two of them had quite a shouting match in front of the entire plane, with this fellow explaining how he resented having these kind of pictures foisted upon him and his family in a situation in which they were a captive audience. "What am I supposed to do," he asked the captain, "get off the plane?" Finally, one of the passengers suggested that a vote be taken as to whether to show the movie, and interestingly, the majority voted to do without the movie.

That Jew made his own sealed room. We have to ask ourselves: What is our sealed room?

A suggestion. Many of us have, from time to time, considered moving to *Eretz Yisrael*. Now, as you all know, before contemplating moving to *Eretz Yisrael,* modern Israel is no utopia, and both within the religious community and in the society at large, there is a great deal that is very hard for the average Orthodox Jew from America to adjust to. Certainly, most of the media and much of the population there slavishly apes all the most degenerate aspects of American popular culture. But at the same time, it is clear that religious Jews in *Eretz Yisrael* have been much more successful than we have in cutting themselves off from the surrounding society and in sheltering their homes from its pernicious influences. There is an intensity and purity of religious life that we can only envy. So in weighing whether or not to move to *Eretz Yisrael,* this should be one of the important considerations.

Lastly, we must pray for the Redemption and not let ourselves imagine for one second that all is well for us in America. It is not. Two hundred years ago, Rabbi Chaim of Volozhin foresaw that America would be the last way station of exile on our way back to *Eretz Yisrael.* But that vision gave him no joy, only bitter tears, because he realized that this last and final exile was going to cost us dearly. Whether he could see a 60 percent rate of intermarriage I do not know, but he knew that the cost was going to be very high.

So the next time we say in our *Shemoneh Esrai,* "Let the seed of David blossom forth because for Your Redemption we hope all the day," let us mean it. Let us pray with the realization that this *galus* is extracting too high a toll from us, that it is becoming increasingly impossible to live the lives of purity and sanctity for which Hashem designated us from the very beginning. And if we *daven* as if we meant it — not with the feeling that all is well with us here in America — maybe then we will be privileged to see *Mashiach* soon in our days.

Dealing with Affluence, or, What's Wrong With a $2 Million Birthday Party

Not very long ago, Malcolm Forbes Sr., the late publisher of Forbes Magazine, made a seventieth birthday party for himself. This was not just any birthday party — not even by the standards of the *simchas* we have grown used to. Forbes did not make it in America where he lived, but instead chose a more exotic locale — Morocco — to which he flew such celebrity friends as Henry Kissinger and Walter Cronkite. In all, the affair was estimated to cost at least $2 million.

The apparent self-indulgence of throwing a $2 million party for oneself set off a torrent of self-righteous tongue-clucking in the popular press. But we have to ask ourselves: What was so terrible? Here was a man who made his money in an honest manner, who was known to contribute generously to charity. If he wanted to have a gala birthday bash, what's wrong with that? To answer the question of what was wrong with Malcolm Forbes' birthday party — or at least what would have been wrong if his name had been Morris Farbstein — I want to examine the subject of affluence through the eyes of *Chazal*.

❧ "IT'S NOT YOURS"

If one wants to understand anything in the Torah at its most fundamental level, one has to look at the first place that particular subject is mentioned in the Torah. The first test of affluence mentioned in the Torah is in connection with the departure of *bnei Yisrael* (the children of Israel) from Egypt on their way to *Eretz Yisrael*. *Bnei Yisrael* were commanded to go to their Egyptian neighbors and ask them for all their vessels of silver and gold in fulfillment of the promise Hashem made 430 years earlier to Avraham that his offspring would leave bondage with great wealth.

The Torah uses a surprising terminology when describing this command: *Bnei Yisrael* are told that they should "borrow" these vessels from their Egyptian neighbors. This language is difficult to understand. The Jewish people had no intention of returning to Egypt; they weren't borrowing these vessels, they were taking them. So why does the Torah command them to "borrow"?

The Gerrer Rebbe answered that the borrowing was not from the Egyptians — as far as they were concerned all the gold and silver was being taken permanently, as payment. The borrowing was from Hashem. At the very moment that *Klal Yisrael* obtained great wealth for the first time, Hashem stressed that their money did not belong to them. All that wealth was borrowed from Hashem, to whom all gold and silver ultimately belongs.

The message that all we possess belongs to Hashem is reiterated in numerous mitzvos in the Torah. The entire observance of *shemittah*, during which we allow the land to lie fallow for an entire year, emphasizes that Hashem is the owner of *Eretz Yisrael* and we only use the Land subject to His Will. Similarly, we cannot sell land in *Eretz Yisrael* in perpetuity because it does not belong to us; we lack sufficient ownership of the Land to be able to sell or give it to another Jew forever. In the *Yovel* (Jubilee Year), the Land returns to its original owner.

Once we recognize that we are not the real owners of our wealth our perspective is radically changed. If we really believe that we hold the money in trust for Hashem, our first question concerning all our wealth must be: What does Hashem want me to do with this?[1] And when we ask ourselves that question, it will be impossible for us to explain why Hashem wants us to spend $2 million on a day of extravagance.

There is a terrifying *Yerushalmi* in *Shekalim* that teaches us how much thought must be put into the question: How does Hashem want me to spend my money? One day Rav Chama and Rav passed a magnificent synagogue in Lod. Rav Chama said: "How much wealth did our ancestors invest here." To which Rav replied: "How many lives were sunk into the ground here? Were there not any Torah scholars whom they could have supported with all the money they wasted on these expensive buildings?" Rav Chama saw how great had been the material sacrifice of all those who contributed to building a

---

1. Interestingly, the prohibition against cheating in business is found in *Behar*, the same Torah portion that deals with the laws of *shemittah* and *yovel*. Both *shemittah* and *yovel*, as we have seen, emphasize that Hashem is the ultimate owner of everything we possess. Once that perspective is ingrained in us, cheating to gain a few more dollars becomes unthinkable.

beautiful synagogue to honor Hashem, and thought of the nobility of their sacrifice. But even in expenditures spent beautifying a *shul,* Rav saw a misappropriation of the funds entrusted to them by Hashem tantamount to murder.

What should they have done with the money? They should have opened up another yeshivah or Bais Yaakov; they should have paid *rebbeim* more so that they could remain in *chinuch* (education) without worrying whether they would be able to marry off their children.

❧ YOU CAN'T TAKE IT WITH YOU

Earlier we discussed *Klal Yisrael's* first experience of wealth: the collecting of the gold and silver from their Egyptian neighbors. Interestingly, Moshe *Rabbeinu* did not join with the rest of *bnei Yisrael* in collecting his neighbors' vessels. While the people were accumulating vast wealth, he was gathering the bones of Yosef *Hatzaddik* for removal from Egypt, as Yosef had requested just before he died.

The *Midrash* comments: "Behold, the wisdom (חכמתו) and goodness (חסידותו) of Moshe *Rabbeinu.*" It is not hard to understand the reference to Moshe's goodness, but why was this incident chosen as a prime illustration of his wisdom?

But if we consider *Chazal's* definition of a wise man — i.e., one who sees the long-range consequences of his actions — we can understand why the *Midrash* praises Moshe *Rabbeinu* for his wisdom. For what Moshe saw was that you can't take it with you. The only thing that remains with us at the end of our 120 years is the mitzvos we do. Moshe's great wisdom was that he maintained this long-term perspective all the time. He never lost sight of the future.

Rabbeinu Bachye in *Parshas Tetzaveh* describes a custom of the righteous men of France, who used to have the coffin in which they were buried made from their dining room tables. In that way they demonstrated that nothing remains with a person from all his striving other than the mitzvos he does, many of them around the dining room table — including inviting guests, feeding the poor, and inviting those without family or friends to share his table.

Rabbi Chaim Volozhin used to give the following parable concerning the people of a certain city called Luz. The *Midrash* tells us that the Angel of Death had no power in Luz. Anyone in Luz who became weary of life had to leave Luz in order for the Angel of Death to take him. Accordingly, the people of Luz lived extremely long lives. One day someone from Luz met a normal mortal. He asked the outsider what kind of house he lived in, and was amazed to discover the amount of effort put into ensuring that the house was beautiful and sturdy. "When we build a house," the man from Luz told him, "we build it to last hundreds of years. But you're here for such a short time that your houses are really more like temporary dwellings. You might as well use orange crates."

Next the man from Luz wanted to hear about the nature of the clothing worn outside Luz. He assumed that given the short time for which they need their clothes, people would be content with fig leaves or the like. Again he was amazed to hear that contrary to his expectations, people spend vast amounts of time and money to make sure that their clothes were the latest style.

A few summers back, our family took a car trip through New England, and one of the places we visited was Newport, Rhode Island. Basically, there are two things to see in Newport: the Touro Synagogue (to which we shall return later) and the grand mansions built as summer homes by the super-rich around the turn of the century. Of these, the one built by railroad magnate Cornelius Vanderbilt is perhaps the most impressive. The

Breakers, as it is called, took four years to build and no expense was spared. Artisans from France and Italy were brought in. Apparently the old robber baron felt the need to demonstrate to the world that he was a man who appreciated culture and beauty. In any event, The Breakers was completed in 1896, and Cornelius Vanderbilt spent one summer in it before suffering a stroke that fall. He never made it back to this monument to his discriminating taste, never again savored the awe of those who came to visit his tribute to himself. All he left was a classic example of the old adage: You can't take it with you.

⚘ KEEP YOUR EYE ON THE GOAL

Since we are living on borrowed time with borrowed money, we have to focus constantly on our real goal so that we not only answer the question "What does Hashem want me to do with my money?" but also, "What does He want me to do with my life?" The two are closely related. So often in our pursuit of money we lose all sight of what our lives are supposed to be about. In the third paragraph of *Krias Shema,* which we recite twice a day, we say, "And do not stray after your heart and after your eyes . . . so that you may remember and perform all My commandments." *Sefer HaChinuch* interprets the straying after your heart and eyes as referring to all the attractions and desires of the physical world.

By seeking to fulfill all our material desires, the verse tells us, we forget G-d's mitzvos. We cannot have both at the same time; we cannot revel in our affluence without having it affect our perspective. We cannot make ever more elaborate weddings without losing our focus on the mitzvos. That little internal gyroscope that keeps a Jew guided towards Hashem's mitzvos stops functioning as life becomes increasingly centered on ever more lavish houses, more expensive vacations. That is not, Hashem tells us, what I put you in the world for.

And the Morris Farbsteins of the world, if not the Malcolm Forbeses, cannot afford to forget this.

We live in a society predicated on helping us to lose our focus. Just in case our own physical desires were not enough, we have entire industries devoted to conjuring up new desires, to convincing us that we are not really living if we don't have Product X. I recently ran across the following ad in a leading Jewish periodical:

> At last, glatt kosher venison. Culled from our very private source of farmed deer and slaughtered in accordance with the strictest of religious laws. Prepared by our chef in several delightful ways amidst a setting of luxury and utmost elegance. Where elegance and comfort combine to make your meal truly memorable.

Now I have nothing against venison *per se,* though I must admit to having lived a fairly happy life thus far without ever having tasted it. But it seems to me that precisely to the extent that venison, eaten amidst luxury and elegance, becomes for us something "truly memorable," will Hashem's commandments become less truly memorable.

Somebody recently told me that people are spending a thousand dollars on their bathroom fixtures. For what? Does the water come out different from a thousand dollar fixture than from a hundred dollar fixture? Whether it's the latest in bathroom fixtures or venison, these ads appeal to the Malcolm Forbes in us, to the part of us that would like to stop worrying about what the *Ribbono shel Olam* wants.

In order to keep our focus, we have to keep asking ourselves: Are we consumers or are we being consumed? Is the house I'm building becoming too important in my life? Am I spending all my time thinking about the fixtures, recessed lighting, etc? Is the *bar mitzvah* becoming too big a deal? Are my thoughts on the seating and the menu or on preparing my son for the yoke of mitzvos? And most importantly, is my career or business taking over my life? Am I being consumed by making money I'll never be able to spend on children I never see?

A few years ago, we were in *Eretz Yisrael* for the first time. We visited a family living on the West Bank. The children kept asking: "What's life like in America?" Finally, their mother, who gave up the luxuries of America for the hard life of the West Bank, told them, "By them the main thing is shopping. Get up in the morning, eat, and go out shopping. Return home, eat a little bit more, and again go out shopping. Shopping, shopping, shopping." It's become a joke in our house. Whenever I see my wife going out, I ask her, "Where are you going?" And she replies, "Shopping, shopping, shopping."

One of the Seven Wonders of Baltimore, where I live, is the Owings Mill Mall, popularly known as the Western Mall. Instead of praying at the Western Wall, people seem to worship at the Western Mall.

We are digging ourselves ever deeper into this rut of consumerism. What for us are luxuries — something you treat yourself to as a reward for hard work — are our children's necessities. A woman told me recently that a little girl was in her house and she wanted to call her mother. Someone was on the phone, so the little girl asked, "Where's the second line?" It never occurred to her that there could be a house with only one telephone line.

Admittedly this may not be the best example. For many people who run businesses from the home or who have large families, a second line may be a necessity not a luxury. But we have to know that whatever we have becomes for our children the minimum standard of living. We recently moved into a new home, and among the other things involved was purchasing a new refrigerator. The appliance salesman offered us a good buy on one that had all the features we needed — plus an automatic icemaker. There is no question that, though unnecessary, an icemaker is a convenience, especially if it's free. No more going to the refrigerator and finding that someone had put back an empty ice tray. I must admit that I am very fond of my new luxury item — but I also know that my children are going to *need* an icemaker; for them, it will not be just a luxury. "What's an ice tray?" they will want to know.

✎ USE IT, DON'T FLAUNT IT

I do not want to be misunderstood. The Torah does not teach us that we must take vows of poverty or that every physical enjoyment of this world is a bad thing. On the contrary, the Torah recognizes that a certain amount of freedom from financial worry, a certain minimum standard of living, is necessary for us to focus properly on the spiritual tasks at hand. Having too little can consume us as well and prevent us from having time to think about anything other than where the next meal is coming from.

The *Mishnah* in *Yoma* (52b) tells us that as the *Kohen Gadol* was leaving the Holy of Holies on Yom Kippur he recited a short prayer. What was this short prayer? In the *Gemara* (53b), the *Amoraim* discuss what the prayer was. One says: If this year is a hot one, let there be plenty of rain. Another says: Do not let Your people need to seek a livelihood from one another and do not heed the prayers of the wayfarers [who pray that no rain will fall while they are traveling from place to place].

The *Gemara* is astounding. We would expect that the *Kohen Gadol* at this moment would be concentrating on the spiritual needs of the Jewish people. But we hear not one word about mitzvos, about educating our children to follow in Hashem's ways, about *Mashiach.* Just about the rain. At that moment, the *Kohen Gadol* seems to be thinking about nothing other than earning a livelihood.

The explanation is that the *Kohen Gadol* was indeed thinking about spiritual matters. Let them have rain, he pleaded with the *Ribbono shel Olam,* so that they can do what they are supposed to do, so that they can be what they are supposed to be — *Klal Yisrael,* a nation focused on Hashem and the study of His Torah.

But if we are not proscribed from acquiring wealth, we are nevertheless constrained in how we use our money. One of the first of those rules is : Do not flaunt your wealth. Do not flaunt it in front of your fellow Jews and do not flaunt it in front of the gentiles.

When we ostentatiously display our money in front of our fellow Jews, we can destroy lives. If a wealthy person makes a wedding on a grand scale, he raises the standards of the whole community. Soon everyone else has to follow suit on a similar scale, and people are mortgaging their lives, their futures, just to make a wedding for their child. We all have heard stories of educators who, after years in *chinuch,* decided they had to leave it for a more lucrative profession so that their childrens' weddings would not be an embarrassment, so that they would not be marked as *shleppers* and have-nots.

Talk to anyone from abroad who comes to an American wedding for the first time and you will find that there is one thing he can not stop talking about: the smorgasbord. His first question is: Hasn't anybody here eaten all week that they need a sixteen-dish smorgasbord? But that's the standard.

What we do not realize when we make this kind of wedding is that we may be destroying our children's education with it.

We may be driving some poor *rebbi* into a career in computers even though he loves teaching.

And when we flaunt our money, we leave ourselves open to the *ayin hara* (the Evil Eye). If you become the talk of the community, inevitably that is going to create a great deal of jealousy. That, in turn, causes you to be judged more strictly in Heaven. If people are jealous of you, the Heavenly tribunal starts appraising you in a different light above, and the question that they will be asking is: Does he really deserve that money? Is he using it for the purposes for which it was "loaned" to him? How many of us can withstand that kind of scrutiny? If we can't, we shouldn't make a show of wealth.

And equally important: Don't flaunt it in front of your gentile neighbors. We live in the most generous and hospitable host country of the exile, but we must never forget that it is still a Christian country and act accordingly. The *Kli Yakar* writes on the words, "Turn yourself northward (צפונה)" (Devarim 2:3) that we should understand the word צפון as meaning hidden. If a Jew is blessed with wealth, says the *Kli Yakar*, he should hide it from the gentiles. We live in the Exile of Edom, which means that we live among the descendants of Esav, and Esav has a long memory: He remembers that Yaakov stole the blessings from him and continues to hate Yaakov and his descendants.

Our ancestors knew this. Jewish communities — whether in Rome or in Salonika or in Prague — had sumptuary laws, laws against conspicuous consumption. When the *Noda b'Yehudah* was the *rav* in Prague he instituted rules about the size of *bar mitzvahs*. And these were not vague injunctions not to spend so much; they were detailed prescriptions of precisely how much could be spent. For a *bar mitzvah*, no more than ten people could be invited, and entertainment was out. The type of food that could be served — down to the type of fish — was strictly regulated according to the amount of taxes that a person paid.

If you visit the Touro Synagogue in Newport, Rhode Island, the oldest synagogue in continuous use in America, you will notice two things of interest. First, you will not be able to find it without looking for the sign. The building from the outside is completely nondescript; it blends right in with the surrounding buildings, not calling attention to itself. The founders were descendants of Jews who had been forced to flee Spain, with only the possessions on their back. In Spain, the Jews had attained both wealth and influence; the most trusted advisor of King Ferdinand and Queen Isabella at the time of the Inquisition was the Abarbanel. Yet all their wealth and influence did not protect them because they had not absorbed the *Kli Yakar's* warning to hide their wealth and had instead insisted on flaunting it. Their descendants remembered this lesson when they came to the New World.

The second interesting thing about the Touro Synagogue is that under the *bimah* from which the Torah is read is a trap door with a tunnel leading out of the *shul.* Those children of refugees from Spain had also learned that existence in exile can never be taken for granted. No matter how secure your position, be prepared to flee for your life at an instant's notice.

The *Noda b'Yehudah* saw what these elaborate celebrations were doing to the community, and he put a stop to it. We have to do the same. We should pressure the communal rabbis to issue *takannos* (legislative decrees) and put a stop to this extravagance. It is draining our resources, driving our best educators into other fields, incurring jealousy among Jew and gentile alike. It is a danger to our national health, and we must find ways to stop it.

We in America today live in a manner that is a complete anomaly in terms of the historical experience of the Jewish people in exile. If one had to identify a single constant through-out the last two thousand years of exile, it would be the almost unceasing poverty in which the vast majority of Jews all over the globe have lived. Our great-grandparents came from *shtetls* in Europe in which the majority of the Jews depended on charity at Pesach time for the bare necessities. If you look at Roman Vishniac's haunting photographs of pre-war Poland, you will see a little girl forced to spend the entire winter in bed because she lacked shoes and could not even bear to touch her feet to the frozen floor.

Today in America we live in a degree of comfort that would have been unimaginable for any of our ancestors, and we must ask ourselves the question: Why is this exile different? What has changed?

The *Sforno* explains the verse, "Yeshurun grew fat and kicked" (Devarim 32:15), to refer to acquiring the taste for material pleasures. *Klal Yisrael,* he says, is blessed with a cer-tain refinement, a certain delicacy of perception, that is lost by too great an involvement in the pleasures of the world. Even the most refined sensibility grows coarse when surrounded by excess.

What is the corrective for having grown dulled and coarse? Exile. Poverty, persecution, and deprivation are Hashem's ways of refining us, of returning to us our sensitivity to spiritual mat-ters. That is why poverty has always been the hallmark of exile.

If today we live amidst material plenty, even in exile, it must be we have reached the end of exile. We have paid the price; we have been cleansed of our coarseness.[2] The pogroms, the

---

2. This explanation of our present affluence is based on a talk I once heard from Rabbi Elya Svei.

Chmielnicki massacres, the Holocaust were — Hashem is telling us — enough. We have been purified and placed at the threshold of the coming of *Mashiach*. We in America have seen our most powerful enemy, a country feared around the world, simply implode before our very eyes, destroyed by the evil at its core. Go to the local *beis medrash,* and you will find newly arrived Russian Jews learning there — Jews who were thought to be permanently lost to our people just a few years ago.

All that remains for us is to demonstrate that we have inculcated the lessons of exile, to show *Hakadosh Boruch Hu* that we have regained the spiritual sensitivity that is ours as an inheritance from the forefathers. Hashem wants to give us another chance; He wants to bring us back to our Land to live fully in accord with His will.

America, Rabbi Chaim Volozhin foresaw nearly two hundred years ago, would be the final way station of Torah prior to our return to *Eretz Yisrael.* The material plenty with which we live today is for only one purpose: to test us. Prior to returning us to our Land, Hashem must be sure that we will not again allow plenitude to cause us to lose our sense of His immediate presence.

We have come full circle since Yeshurun choked on its own material plenty and rebelled. May we merit to pass the test of affluence so that we can see *Mashiach* speedily in our days.

The Orthodox Woman
in the Workplace

I t is not without a fair degree of trepidation that I approach this topic. By comparison, marital harmony [*Shalom Bayis*] and the education of our children, for instance, are easy topics: Everyone is for *Shalom Bayis*. But the subject of Orthodox women working is one that excites strong feelings and often sharp disagreement.

On the one hand, it is an undeniable fact that a large percentage of Orthodox women today work outside the home, and that situation is not likely to change any time in the near future. On the other hand, the dangers entailed by the exposure to the marketplace are also fairly clear. Thus one who writes or speaks on this topic must steer between criticizing a situation that he cannot change, on the one hand, and of appearing to give a blanket condonation and *post facto* justification for what is a problematic reality, on the other.

I do not wish to be accused of hypocrisy on this topic, so in the interests of full disclosure, I should note that my wife works outside the home and has for most of our married life. I hope no one will come to Baltimore and be surprised that Mrs. Frand works, in light of anything I may write on this topic.

For the last two hundred years at least, an Orthodox woman working outside the home has not been an anomaly. The *Chafetz Chaim's* wife ran a store to help support the family and so did the *Chazon Ish's* wife so that he could learn without distraction. "*Eishes Chayil*," which we sing every Friday night, describes a woman who is compared to a merchant ship. So the Book of *Mishlei* itself apparently contemplates a woman working in some fashion outside of the home. One of the *Ramban's* principles for interpreting *Tanach* is that there is no allegory that is not true at its simplest level of understanding. Thus if "*Eishes Chayil*" uses the business acumen of a woman as a metaphor for some more spiritual quality, it remains true that such business acumen is itself a praiseworthy quality.

At the same time, it would be too facile to say that if the *Chafetz Chaim's* Rebbetzin worked, then our doing so is unproblematic. The world of the *Chafetz Chaim's* time is a very different one from our own, and running a store in the tiny *shtetl* of Radin is a far cry from working in the offices of billion-dollar corporations.

If I were to take a poll of Orthodox women in their 20's, 30's, and 40's, I am confident that a relatively small percentage had mothers who worked outside the home. Today, however, probably a majority of women in this age group work. What has changed?

First, for many couples today the wife's working is an economic necessity. Few mothers of today's young Orthodox women had husbands who learned in *kollel* until their late 20's or even into their 30's. But that is commonplace today, and as a consequence the wife is often the primary breadwinner. In addition, many have large families, and it takes a great deal of money to raise a large family between school tuition, medical care, insurance, food, orthodontia, camp, etc.

Nor can we discount the influence of the society in which we live. The media today tends to portray women who stay home and raise the children as somehow substandard creatures lacking both intellectual ability and ambition. Ask a woman who does so what she does and she is likely to answer with embarrassment, "I'm *just* a housewife." That "just" says it all. I read recently about a woman who had to give up her job after the birth of a child. For months after the birth, she was afraid to leave her home for fear that she would have to fill out a form with a box for occupation and write "housewife."

Modern society tends to ascribe importance to jobs in terms of how much one is paid to do them. It is no accident that the system of public education is on the verge of collapse. Teachers are among the lowest paid professionals, which unfortunately reflects the fact that we do not care that much about the education of our young. Way above teachers on the totem pole are lawyers. Many good lawyers earn incomes well into six figures.

Higher still on the salary scale are the CEOs of large corporations. With bonuses, which seem to come whether the company does well or poorly, many of them make over a million dollars a year. And it is understandable that the CEO of Black and Decker should be the highest paid executive in my city of Baltimore. After all, where would we be without our Dustbusters? But we still have not reached the highest echelon. In Baltimore, as in many cities, that's reserved for the sports and entertainment heroes. For providing the city of Baltimore with one of baseball's best shortstops, and certainly its most durable, Cal Ripken Jr. is paid over five million dollars a year.

At the extreme other end of the totem pole, in dead last place, are the housewives. They receive absolutely nothing for their services, even though they are on 24-hour-a-day call. Given that status is connected with the amount earned, it is no wonder that such leading feminists as Betty Friedan found such a ready audience a quarter of a century ago for her attack on the "drudgery" of housework.

Over 20 years ago, at the height of the tumultuous '60's and '70's, Rabbi Yaakov Weinberg told me that many of the movements that were then attracting so many adherents posed little threat to the Orthodox world because their non-Torah perspective was so obvious. But, he warned, the women's liberation movement would invade our world too, including the Bais Yaakovs, and its effects would prove both pervasive and pernicious, for the movement denigrates the value of being a wife and mother. And when Jewish women start thinking of being a mother as something unelevated, as something unworthy of their talents and energies, we are in very deep trouble.

There is a terrible price to be paid for the denigration of the role of Jewish wife and mother. When King David brought the Ark of the Covenant to Jerusalem, he danced and cavorted in front of the Ark. His wife Michal, the daughter of King Shaul, looked out the window and saw the king dancing, and he became debased in her heart (Shmuel II 6:16). Michal met him as he returned home and told him sarcastically that he had dishonored his position by behaving in such a manner "in front of the maidservants of his servants ..." (*ibid.* v.20). David was angry with Michal for having referred to the wives of his servants by the derogatory term of maidservants (אמהות). He told her, "... and of the maidservants of whom you have spoken, through them will I be honored." The entire incident concludes with the statement that Michal did not have any child until the day of her death, implying that she died in childbirth. (There are differing opinions in the *Gemara* as to whether she had previously had children. Compare *Sanhedrin* 19b and 21a.)

The *Midrash* states explicitly that Michal was punished for the way she spoke to David with not having any children prior to dying in childbirth. Rabbi Meir Bergman, in *Sha'arei Orah*, explains that for despising a mother's work and describing it as maid's work, Michal never experienced motherhood.

We should not think, however, the entire issue of women working has been thrust upon us only due to economic necessity and societal mores. It has been observed that there is a recurrent pattern in the Orthodox world of the solution to one problem bringing in its wake a slew of new problems. The Bais Yaakov movement might serve as a case in point. In the late 19th century, universal education became widespread. As a consequence, religious girls, who had no available school system, were going to public schools and studying the humanities and sciences. Their largely uneducated mothers ceased to be any kind of role models for girls' education in the best gymnasia. It was not uncommon in the best of families for the girls to sit on Shabbos writing term papers while their fathers were studying the *parashah* with their brothers.

Moreover, there were increasingly fewer girls willing to marry *yeshiva bochurim*. I once met an old Jew from Bialystock. He asked me what I did, and I told him that I give a *shiur* in yeshiva. When he heard that, he immediately wanted to meet my wife. After I introduced them, he was simply amazed that any apparently normal, presentable young woman had been willing to marry someone who learned in yeshiva. In his day in Bialystock, the only girls who would consider a *yeshiva bochur* were those who could not find any other kind of husband.

So this was the situation that Bais Yaakov came to remedy. A seamstress in Cracow had the vision to realize that *Klal Yisrael* as the *Am HaTorah* would soon cease to exist without girls committed to its perpetuation. And that seamstress, Sarah Schenirer, brought her plan for girls' education to the Gerrer Rebbe, and he lent the full force of his immense prestige to the Bais Yaakov movement.

Bais Yaakov unquestionably saved the yeshiva world, but not without its costs. In the process of providing girls with a deep Torah education, we whetted their appetites for study in a way that cannot simply be turned off at 18 or 19 when they finish seminary. Until then, they have been involved, often no less intensely than their male counterparts, in the most stimulating, the most profound study that there is, and it is impossible for them to simply cut themselves off from that. They look at their husbands, and they realize that in many areas of Torah study their knowledge often exceeds that of the men to a considerable extent, and they are unwilling and unable to remain content without further intellectual stimulation either within Torah studies or in other areas.

In other words, we have created a need for intellectual fulfillment that cannot in many cases be met by being a wife and mother alone. If that were not enough, we also tell our young women that they should acquire a further education — whether it be to go into *chinuch,* or computers, or to be a dental technician — in order to support a *yungerman* in *kollel.* We have in effect thrown them out into the workplace.

THE LURKING DANGERS

Prior to her violation by Shechem, Dinah the daughter of Leah is described as going out to view the daughters of the land. *Chazal* comment on the fact that she is described as the daughter of Leah and not as the daughter of Yaakov. They connect her going out to the going out of her mother Leah. Leah met Yaakov in the field and told him that she had exchanged her son Reuven's *dudaim* for the right to have him remain in her tent that night. Plainly, *Chazal* condemn Dinah for her eagerness to leave the protection of her father's house to become acquainted with those living around them. But if so, what is the connection to Leah? Leah's going out on that occasion is considered praiseworthy: Yissachar, the tribe of Torah scholars, was her reward for having traded the *dudaim* for Rachel's night with Yaakov. Indeed, the self-denial needed to become a Torah scholar was an inheritance to Yissachar from his mother Leah, who humiliated herself by going out to the field to bring Yaakov to her tent.

We are left, then, with a paradox: The same act of Leah's which produced Yissachar also led to an immodest act by her daughter Dinah and the terrible consequences that resulted from it. Rabbi Elya Svei once pointed out at an Agudath Israel convention that we see from this *Chazal* that even the most laudable venture out of the home, no matter how praiseworthy the motives, carries with it built-in pitfalls. Reb Elya was certainly not saying that leaving the home is prohibited. After all, Agudath Israel of America — on whose Moetzes Gedolei HaTorah he serves — has a full-scale program to train women as computer programmers. What he was saying is that when a woman leaves the safe confines of her home, she must do so with her eyes open to the dangers involved and exercise extreme caution.

Let me try to paint three scenarios involving women of different ages to give you some picture of what those pitfalls are.

The Orthodox Woman in the Workplace □ 205

Scenario I: A 19-year-old girl fresh out of seminary is encouraged by her teachers to find a good job that will allow her to support a husband in learning. She finds an entry level job in a large company. Her intelligence, honesty, and dedication win her a number of promotions. Three years later, she is earning $30-35,000 a year.

In the meantime, she has lost interest in living in a two-bedroom apartment in Lakewood and struggling on a much smaller income. She is no longer the same shy Bais Yaakov girl who left seminary three years ago. The clothes she wears are different — perhaps she has even been afflicted with "designer disease." We are not talking about immodest clothes, but the change in her attitude toward the values of the seminary is obvious to even the most casual observer.

Certainly the transformation I am describing will not happen to everyone. Nor will all parents consider it necessarily a tragedy; some may feel that their daughters should be exposed to the broader world. But know that such changes are common. Go in with your eyes open.

Scenario II: Now we are talking about a woman who is a bit older, between 25 and 30, securely anchored in her marriage, her family, her community. She has to face a different problem: guilt. She has to watch her children cry in the morning as she pulls out of the driveway, listen to their constant questions about when she is coming home, endure their complaints about their babysitters. Over and over each day, she has to ask herself: Am I doing the right thing?

I read once about a woman who was a regional supervisor for AT&T, who was expressing the sadness that often goes with the long hours away from home, such as the time she called her housekeeper from an out-of-town business trip to be told that her baby had just taken his first steps. No matter how vital, how holy the work, it can never provide complete protection against that sadness. Rebbetzin Kaplan, the founder of the first Bais Yaakov Seminary in America, used to say, "I wish *Eliyahu HaNavi* would visit and tell me, 'Vichna Kaplan, you are doing the right thing.' " But that visit never came, and she, and most others in her position, had to struggle with the uncertainty and guilt.

Scenario III: A middle-aged working woman whose children are older and do not return home until the late afternoon. She does not have to feel that she is cheating them in the same way a woman with younger children does. Her problem is different: She is expected to be a superwoman. Even though half her waking hours are spent at work and commuting back and forth, she is still expected to be the complete wife and mother making sure the larder is always full, the shirts ironed, the cabinets clean, the children well dressed and well mannered. In short, she is expected upon her return from work to slip into a phone booth — à la Clark Kent — and come out wearing an apron proclaiming "Super Mom."

Is the following item from *The New York Times* any surprise?

> *While women's progress on the job is visible and public, men and women are sorting out the implications in the privacy of their homes and questioning the price they have paid for the change. Americans, both women and men, say they are unhappy about the toll on their family and personal lives. Since the publication of Betty Friedan's The Feminine Mystique, women who work outside the home report that their children and their marriages are being shortchanged, and they lament having too little time for themselves.*

Nor can we ignore the inherent dangers of the workplace. Our standards of modesty and propriety in speech and action are far from those of the society at large. Flirtatious repartee, suggestive comments, off-color jokes are commonplace.

The Orthodox Woman in the Workplace □ 207

Even given the considerably looser standards of contemporary society, 15% of women in a recent poll by *Working Woman Magazine* reported that they had been the victims of sexual harassment in the office, and other polls place the figure at twice that or higher.

Of course not all contact between the sexes in the office takes the form of sexual harassment. There is also a great deal of camaraderie. Men and women are thrown together in close contact; they work together under pressure on big projects, the outcome of which often becomes — at least for the moment — the most important thing in their lives. Everyone is well dressed, seen at their best, and, unfortunately, women are often treated better and with more respect than in their own homes. All this threatens marriages.

⊷ A FEW QUESTIONS

Now that we understand some of the dangers and problems inherent in work outside the home, we are in a position to analyze anew some of the original justifications for such work. The first was economic necessity — whether it be the cost of children's school tuition or maintaining a son or son-in-law in *kollel* — and that is certainly a compelling and desirable reason. But given the downside risks, it behooves us to ask whether the motivation is necessity, or a rationalization for the pursuit of luxury. Not that every desire for a somewhat higher lifestyle has to be condemned, but the unseen deduction on the pay check must be recognized. At the very least, a job outside the house will frequently entail leaving children in the care of others, being harried and hassled, and exposure to the often unsavory aspects of the American workplace. So if the reason for working is an enhanced lifestyle, this must be balanced against more time with the family and the dangers involved.

Next we mentioned the desire for intellectual stimulation

and fulfillment. Though, as we have seen, much of that desire is culturally determined, it is none the less real for all that. Human beings are products of the society in which they live. Here too it is necessary, however, to strip away some of the illusions. Jobs can quickly become very tedious and boring. They are as frequently mind numbing as mind expanding. We would, for instance, think that being a college professor is the pinnacle of intellectual work. Yet I recently read of a college English professor who found the reality of term papers and tests and correcting garbled syntax was a far cry from the career of being "happily embalmed in the formaldehyde of academia" she had anticipated. So she took the dramatic step of quitting to do something she found at once more meaningful, more stimulating, and more enjoyable than teaching: raising her children.

If it is intellectual stimulation that is needed, then the 15 years of intensive Torah education that most of today's Orthodox girls have received should provide the tools. No matter how complete the education, they did not exhaust the limitless sources of intellectual, emotional, and spiritual stimulation in the Torah. Besides studying alone or with a friend, there are today in most major Torah centers shiurim available day and night, and with the wonders of modern technology there is no dearth of material available even for those who cannot attend shiurim in person.

For those who feel the need to "do something," there is no shortage of chesed and communal work to be done. There are help-lines, mikvaos, shuls, yeshivas, and Bais Yaakovs that can all benefit from the assistance of talented volunteers.

Even if the choice is made to enter the marketplace, that does not mean that there are no more questions to be asked. The questions are just beginning. First, there is the question of where and for whom to work. Obviously, working for frum employers, especially Torah institutions and communal organizations, is preferable, and helps to avoid some of the dangers we mentioned. Even with non-religious or gentile employers, the presence of religious co-workers can make an important difference. The presence of others from our background helps us preserve a sense of who we are and serves as an important restraint on temptations to deviate from the standards of modesty with which we grew up.

Questions will arise in the course of any career in the working world, and it is therefore important to find a *rav* or *posek* with whom one feels comfortable discussing the issues involved. He can help in establishing the boundaries and *gedarim* (fences) that a working Orthodox woman needs to establish for herself.

But after all is said and done, and husband and wife have together determined that it is important that she work, she should do so without becoming overwhelmed by guilt. Hashem does not desire guilt-ridden Jews. What He does desire is Jews who are *erlich* and honest — honest in their evaluation of their situation and *erlich* in their work — if that is the decision they make for themselves.

"Necessity is neither praiseworthy nor condemnable," is a frequently quoted maxim in the halachic literature. The only question is what do we do with the situation that has been forced upon us. We will be judged by the limits we set for ourselves. If the working woman is honest with herself and honest in her work, then she is truly worthy of the praise of Shlomo *Hamelech,* היתה כאניות סוחר ממרחק תביא לחמה ...זממה שדה ותקחהו בפרי כפיה נטעה כרם — "She is like a merchant's ships, from afar she brings her sustenance. . . . She envisions a field and buys it, from the fruit of her handiwork she plants a vineyard." For she will be a true *eishes chayil.*

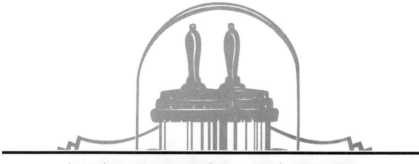

TIMELESS
TOPICS

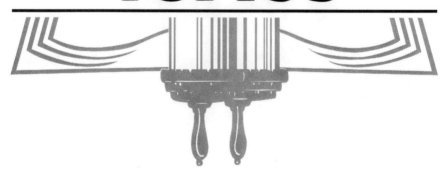

Rebuilding the Bais Hamikdash: What Can We Do?

Imagine that a $10 million building campaign was announced to rebuild the *Bais Hamikdash*. Can anyone doubt that the sum, or even ten times as much, would be raised within hours? Yet, writes the *Chafetz Chaim*, we are not required to spend a penny to rebuild the *Bais Hamikdash* — a building campaign without fundraising! All that is needed is to rectify the sins of *lashon hara* and *sinas chinam* (causeless hatred) for which the second Temple was destroyed — in short, to approach one another in a spirit of peace. And yet, *Mashiach* tarries and the *Bais Hamikdash* continues to lie in ruins, the *Kodesh HaKadoshim* (Holy of Holies) covered by a mosque.

Chazal remind us in numerous subtle and not so subtle ways of the cause for the Temple's destruction. Whenever *Rosh Chodesh* falls on Sunday, the *Haftarah* of the preceding *Shabbos* begins with the words, "Yonasan said to [David], "Tomorrow is the New Moon..." (Shmuel I 20:18). With the exception of these words there is seemingly no other connection between the *Haftarah* and *Rosh Chodesh* the following day, and yet *Chazal* decreed that it would supplant the normal *Haftarah* of the *parashah*. Why?

To answer that question, Rabbi Shimon Schwab noted that in the *Mussaf* of *Rosh Chodesh* we beg Hashem, "May You establish a new Altar in Zion..." When *Rosh Chodesh* is on Sunday, the preceding day's *Haftarah* reminds us why on the morrow we will daven *Mussaf* rather than *bring a Mussaf* offering, why we will pray for the rebuilding of the Altar rather than bring our sacrifices upon one that is already rebuilt. In that *Haftarah* there is a dramatic exchange between King Shaul and his son Yonasan. King Shaul asks at the festive *Rosh Chodesh* meal, "Why has the son of Yishai [i.e., David] not come not yesterday and not today?" A seemingly innocent question, but one that reverberates throughout the generations, for *Mashiach*, too, is referred to as ben Yishai. Why has he not come? For the same reason that David did not come. Just as David did not come due to the causeless hatred that King Shaul had in his illness conceived for him, so his descendant the *Mashiach* does not come because of causeless hatred.

On Tishah B'Av, we read the Book of *Eichah* as part of our mourning over the destruction of the Temple. There the prophet Yirmiyahu cries out, "He filled me with bitterness

(במרורים), sated me with wormwood" (Eichah 3:15). The word מרורים resonates for us and reminds us of Pesach night when we are commanded to eat the Pesach sacrifice together with bitter herbs (מרורים). *Midrash Eichah* makes explicit the connection between Pesach and the mourning of Tishah B'Av: " 'He filled me with bitterness' — this refers to the first day of Pesach; 'sated me with wormwood' — this refers to Tishah B'Av." The Midrash then draws another connection between Pesach and Tishah B'Av: Tishah B'Av is always on the same day of the week as the first day of Pesach.

The message for us is: If Pesach comes and goes, and you still have not absorbed its lesson, then you are guaranteed that Tishah B'Av will remain a night of crying. And what is that lesson? The Gateshead *Mashgiach*, Rabbi Mattisiyahu Solomon, says the lesson is one taught by the two dippings at the *Seder*. Those dippings, the *Ben Ish Chai* explains, are reminders of two historical events — one related to the going down to Egypt and the other to our Redemption from Egypt. The first dipping reminds us of how Yosef's brothers dipped his coat into the blood of a goat and brought it to their father Yaakov. Because of their hatred of their own brother we descended to slavery in Egypt.

The second dipping conveys a similar message by reminding us of an event diametrically opposed to the dipping of Yosef's coat in blood. Just before the Jewish people left Egypt, we were instructed to take a bunch of hyssop and dip it in blood. The bunch (אגודת) of hyssop represents the unity of the Jewish people — the unity that was the precondition for leaving Egypt. According to the Midrash (*Midrash Hillel* p. 127), in addition to not changing their dress or their Jewish names, the Jewish people in Egypt did not speak *lashon hara* about one another. They were thus able to correct the sin of Yosef's brothers, which had brought them to Egypt in the first place. And until we do the same today, we cannot hope to leave our *galus* (exile) behind; and Tishah B'Av will remain a night of crying and mourning.

The *Netziv* describes in more detail the precise nature of the hatred without cause for which the *Bais Hamikdash* was destroyed: "Each person suspected that anyone whose form of yiras Hashem (fear of G-d) was different from his own was a Sadducee and an apikorus." In other words, there was no tolerance for another's approach in service of Hashem, no willingness to admit that there are legitimate Torah approaches and customs different from one's own.

Does this sound hauntingly familiar? I do not know exactly how it was during the time of the *Bais Hamikdash*, but it seems to me that we have raised to a new art form this attitude of dismissiveness to anyone who differs from us ever so slightly.

The truth is that the ability to write other Orthodox Jews off so easily is a luxury that we did not enjoy fifty years ago. Then Torah observance was so weak that if a person was *shomer Shabbos* and kept kosher no more questions were asked — he was an observant Jew. Today the Orthodox world has grown so greatly that we can subdivide ourselves into ever more numerous subgroups, limit ourselves to those ever more identical to ourselves, and still have a community. Intolerance, then, is in part a reflection of our success. Moreover, much of our limiting ourselves to ever narrower groups has to do with our strong determination to shield ourselves and our families from an ever more hedonistic outside society.

And it should be said that tolerance, as practiced in the broader society today, is not a Torah virtue. The easygoing tolerance of "I'm o.k.; you're o.k." has nothing to do with the Torah. That kind of tolerance results from the assumption that all values are subjective, nothing more than each person's personal opinion. In a world in which it is assumed that there is no such thing as objective truth, we are forced to tolerate the next fellow's opinions because there is no ultimate standard to which we can have recourse to decide which opinions are right.

For the Jew who believes that Hashem gave the Torah at

Sinai, such tolerance is impossible. The belief in absolute values given by G-d is the very fundament of our lives. That being the case it cannot — and should not — be easy for us to see someone else being less than careful in a matter of halachah or to hear someone else express false opinions in *hashkafah* (Torah philosophy).

If the Torah nevertheless seeks some form of tolerance from us, it is of a much more complex form: a tolerance that at once assumes that values are objective and yet recognizes that there are seventy faces to the Torah. At the very least, we must learn to approach our fellow Orthodox Jew with what *Chazal* call "the right hand draws near while the left pushes away." The right side in Kabbalah is always the Attribute of Kindness, and it is the stronger side. Thus we must make our fellow Jew first feel our love for him and our desire to draw him near, even as it may sometimes be necessary to push away with the left hand — representing the Attribute of Strict Judgment. At a recent convention of Agudath Israel, the Novominsker Rebbe gave expression to this idea. His subject was attitudes to other observant Jews, and he said:

> Our world, however described — yeshivish, Chassidish, heimish — has become all too eager to denigrate and vilify circles of shomrei Torah and mitzvos with whom we have serious ideological differences. Kanaus leshem Shomayim, or zeal for the sake of Heaven, against our Jewish brothers may be warranted. We feel compelled to speak out of pain and protest. But if that militancy is not mixed with a sense of pain and anguish, and is not coupled with a genuine ahavas Yisrael for Jews who are ma'aminim bnei ma'aminim (believers, the sons of believers) and coupled with a real desire to reach out to them, then our zeal is misplaced and flawed.

Our problem today is that too often it is the right hand that pushes away. If we see others making what appear to us to be mistakes, we do not feel a sense that this is a Jewish brother that we have to help. We are too quick to write off someone who is different from ourselves without giving him a second look.

We do not know how to criticize and disagree without denigrating the entire worth of those we are criticizing. There is an interesting *Midrash* that might help us in this regard. We all know that pigs and camels are unkosher animals: the former because it does not chew its cud; the latter because it does not have a split hoof. The *Midrash* (*Bereishis Rabbah* 32:4), however, notes something interesting. The Torah does not tell us that they are unkosher in the simplest fashion: It does not simply enumerate the trait that makes them unkosher. Rather the Torah begins by describing the trait of *kashrus* that each one possesses. Thus the Torah tells us that *although* the pig has a split hoof, it is nevertheless unkosher, and although the camel chews its cud, it is also unkosher.

Do you hear how the *Ribbono shel Olam* talks about a pig, the animal that epitomizes something *treife* for us? He starts by telling us its positive attribute, that which would make it kosher — if only it possessed the other attribute of *kashrus*.

Frankly, I feel a little hamstrung in getting this message across. The following stories and the reaction to them both bring out the message I am trying to convey and indicate how deep is the resistance.

The first story: More than fifty years ago, the leader of the World Mizrachi Organization, Rabbi Zev Gold, who was also incidentally one of the founders of Mesivta Torah Vodaath, came to Baltimore and stayed with my Rosh Yeshiva, Rabbi Yaakov Yitzchak Ruderman. While in Baltimore, he went one night to speak to a group which included many who were extremely lax in their mitzvah observance. At the end of the meeting, one of the participants asked Rabbi Gold why he was staying with Rabbi Ruderman who was, in the questioner's words, "*nisht ken Mizrachist* — not a follower of Mizrachi." Rabbi Gold answered, "Because with Rabbi Ruderman I have differences over one mitzvah. With you, I have differences over dozens of mitzvos."

That story captured perfectly one of the points I am trying to bring out: Even as we are aware of our differences from our fellow Orthodox Jews, let us just keep in sight how much we have in common. Instead of viewing each other as opponents, let us see each other as natural allies. That is what Rabbi Gold ·was saying: I may differ with Rabbi Ruderman about the mitzvah of settling in *Eretz Yisrael*, but let me not lose sight of the fact that we agree about 612 other mitzvos.

When I mentioned, however, to someone that I intended to tell this story in a public speech, they warned me not to. "No one will hear your point," he pleaded. "The only thing that they'll hear is that Rabbi Ruderman must have supported Mizrachi, because he hosted Rabbi Gold." That comment highlights the problem that I am addressing. As soon as the label Mizrachi was attached, rightly or wrongly, to Rabbi Ruderman's name, many listeners would hear nothing else in the story.

Another story. Same point. In looking for examples of how two Jews holding diametrically opposed viewpoints can show tolerance and respect for one another without compromising their own principles, a number of people suggested that I read about the relationship between Rabbi Yosef Chaim Sonnenfeld, the leader of the fiercely anti-Zionist Eidah Hacharedis community in Jerusalem, and Rabbi Avraham Yitzchak Hakohen Kook, the first Ashkenazi Chief Rabbi of Palestine. Despite the crucial differences between them, the two traveled together in a horse-drawn wagon to different settlements in *Eretz Yisrael* to try to convince the settlers to keep kosher and to observe Shabbos. Even when the dispute between the camp led by Rabbi Kook and that led by Rabbi Yosef Chaim Sonnenfeld was

Rebuilding the Bais Hamikdash: What Can We Do? □ 219

at its most intense, whenever the two of them met at a *sim-chah* they made a point of engaging each other in friendly conversation and demonstrating the mutual esteem in which they held each other.

To me this is a beautiful story. It demonstrates that you can argue with someone, you can be convinced that his way is not only wrong but damaging to *Klal Yisrael,* and yet still view him as a person deserving of respect. In other words, there is a vast distinction between *chilukei deos* (differences of opinion) and *machlokes* (strife). The first is not only inevitable, it is desirable. Ideas are too important to us for the "I'm o.k.; you're o.k." approach. Rabbi Sonnenfeld and Rabbi Kook exemplified this distinction.

But when I mentioned to a colleague that I would be telling this story in a *derashah,* he told me that I would get into trouble for mentioning Rabbi Kook. His view was by no means unique. That's what it has come to, and that is why the *Bais Hamikdash* is not rebuilt. It is risky to mention the name of someone who was a prized *talmid* of *gedolei Yisrael* and was viewed as a *tzaddik* and *gadol b'Torah* even by those of his contemporaries most sharply critical of his views.

✎ TELLING YOUR ALLIES FROM YOUR FOES

How can we learn to work with and appreciate those who may have different approaches to *avodas Hashem* than ourselves? My first suggestion would be to broaden our horizons. We have to realize that Jewish life in America does not end at the Verrazano Bridge and that even Brooklyn extends beyond Ocean Parkway. If we adequately appreciated how far from any connection to Yiddishkeit are 90 percent of American Jews, we would have to think twice before writing off so many of the remaining 10 percent. If we talked to the kiruv workers who are on the frontlines, or if we spent time in Jewish communities outside the "Frum Belt," we would jump for joy and run over and hug every Jew we see who keeps *kashrus*, *taharas hamishpachah*, and Shabbos.

If you are not willing to talk to those in kiruv or to spend a Shabbos in the hinterlands, at least try reading the Sunday *New York Times* wedding announcements once in a while. That itself is an eye-opener. Every single Sunday you can read how our Jewish brothers and sisters are being lost forever. See how much you can take of "Miss Steinberg to wed Mr. O'Connor." And don't just stop at the headlines, go on and see what's important to American Jews today, what it is they want to have reported in *The Times*: The bride is a *magna cumma laude* graduate of Yale and is an associate with the law firm of Dewey Ballantine; the groom's father is a senior vice-president with Exxon Corporation. Then go on and read about how Rabbi Shoshana Cohen officiated together with Father Timothy O'Brien. But don't stop there. At the end of one recent piece, the Jewish bride described her mother's reaction when she brought her gentile boyfriend home for the first time. "My mother's first question was: 'What's his Zodiac sign'?"

That is the situation we find ourselves in today. Not so long ago Jewish parents sat *shivah* when their child intermarried. Their only advice to their children going off to college was: "Date Jewish." Today, a parent's first question is: "What's his Zodiac?" In such a world, can we really afford to write off another observant Jew because he wears a white shirt and not a striped one, or because he wears a *kippah sruga* and not a hat?

Recently I was discussing this topic with a rabbi I happened to meet at a wedding, and he made an interesting observation. When two Orthodox Jews of whatever stripe have business dealings together, they have no problem getting along. One could be a "*heimishe Yid*" and the other more modern, but in that setting they each seem to be happy just doing business with another observant Jew. A friend of mine whose child recently underwent major surgery noticed the same phenomenon when he had to spend Shabbos in a hospital. He came into the *shul* and there sitting around talking was a Chassid in *shtreimel* and *kapote*, another Jew in a white Panama hat, and a third wearing a *yarmulka*. A real blend.

If these Jews saw each other on the street, they might not say boo to each other, but in the hospital they sat and had a wonderful time together. The difference in the hospital was that they actually got to know one another. With plenty of time on their hands, they talked to one another. In the course of their conversations, they found out that in all they may disagree on about five or six points, but more important, they also had much in common. They learned that in a Jewish world going to ruin they are allies not enemies.

I once heard from Rabbi Shimon Schwab the following story about the *chasunah* of Rabbi Chaim Shmulevitz and the daughter of the Mirrer Rosh Yeshiva, Rabbi Eliezer Yehudah Finkel. Reb Chaim was a *talmid* of Novordhok Yeshiva, which was famous for its strict *mussar*. At the meal following the *chuppah*, one of the Mirrer *talmidim* stood up and started saying *grammen* (semi-humorous rhymes) as was customary at weddings. But for the Novordhok *bachurim*, the *grammen* were considered excessive levity. Matters became tense, and an argument between the two yeshivos broke out right in the middle of the *chasunah*. Finally, Rabbi Yerucham Levovitz, the great Mirrer *Mashgiach*, was forced to climb onto a chair and start yelling at all those present, "We're all brothers! This is crazy — Mirrers and Novordhokers fighting. We're all brothers!"

Our differences today are often much greater than those between Mir and Novordhok, but we would do well to keep in mind Reb Yerucham's words: "We are all brothers!"

If *Mashiach* still has not come by next Tishah B'Av and we find ourselves once again crying rather than celebrating, there is a *Midrash* in *Midrash Eichah* that we would do well to contemplate. *Chazal* tell us that those living in a generation in which the *Bais Hamikdash* is not rebuilt should view themselves as personally responsible, for they are compared to the generation in which it was destroyed. And this *Midrash* will help us locate the source of our personal and collective failure.

The Book of *Eichah* follows the order of the *aleph-beis*. But after the first chapter, there is one change from the order of the *aleph-bais*: The letter *peh* precedes the letter *ayin*. That inversion of the order of the *aleph-bais*, explains the *Midrash*, is in memory of what the spies did when they spoke with their mouths (פיהם) what they did not see with their eyes (עיניהם).

Does the *Midrash* simply mean that the spies lied? That cannot be, for they did not lie; they reported what they saw. Rather they were punished for what they failed to see and therefore failed to report. Rabbi Shimon Schwab noted that two people can look at the same thing and see something totally different. When Avraham *Avinu* viewed the mountain from afar, he saw the *Shechinah* hovering over the mountain top. And that is what Yitzchak *Avinu* saw as well. But when Avraham asked Yishmael and Eliezer what they saw, they saw nothing but a mountain.

Similarly, the spies saw giants and funerals. But they failed to see the *kedushas ha'Aretz* (the holiness of the Land). They saw what was external and obvious, and failed to perceive what was deeper and eternal. Because they transmitted that superficial view to *Klal Yisrael* and caused them to cry in their tents, we have been crying now for nearly three thousand years.

And we repeat the sin of the spies when we look at another Orthodox Jew and focus only on the externals — on the five percent that is different from us and not the 95 percent we share in common. *Sinas chinam*, *lashon hara*, and *machlokes* (hatred without cause, malicious gossip and dispute) all come from a failure to integrate the lesson of Tishah B'Av, from a failure to look at our fellow Jew and appreciate his *ma'alos* (good attributes), his potential for spiritual greatness. If only we merited to live according to the prayer of Rebbe Elimelech of Lizensk — "Help me, Hashem, to see in my heart the ma'alos of my brothers" — then we will deserve to see the *Bais Hamidkash* rebuilt and the tears of Tishah B'Av turned into tears of rejoicing.

A Jewish Perspective
On Suffering

There are many possible titles for the topic we will be addressing. The traditional shorthand for the subject is "*tzaddik v'ra lo*," or Why Do the Righteous Suffer? In recent years, it has become common to talk about Why Do Bad Things Happen to Good People, after a popular book by the same name. I have chosen neither of these titles for a very simple reason: To ask a question implies that one is going to give an answer. And there is no answer to this question — or rather there is an answer but it is not one that we are capable of apprehending from our current perspective. "Rabbi Yannai said: 'It is not in our power to explain either the tranquility of the wicked or the suffering of the righteous' "(*Pirkei Avos* 4:19).

There will come a time when we will experience the greatest of joys — finding answers for all our doubts. But until Hashem reveals Himself fully to us, we will continue to dwell in darkness, and that means we will never be able to ascertain with any degree of certainty the Divine purpose underlying everything that happens to us.

But if the question, however it is phrased, has no answer, it is nonetheless one that must be addressed. For while we have no answers, we do have approaches that have been handed down to us over the centuries by our Sages, and it is those we will be discussing.

◢ AN AGE-OLD QUESTION

The issue of individual suffering is one that is very much with us today. Modern communications, which have truly created a global village, mean that we are much more aware than formerly of tragedies that happen elsewhere in the world. As a consequence, it seems to us that the number of horrible tragedies is greater than ever.

That is not to imply, of course, that the topic is a new one. It goes back to our very beginning as a people and has occupied the greatest Jewish souls from Moshe on down. After Moshe and Aharon made their first appearance in front of Pharaoh, Pharaoh increased the load on the Jewish people in order that "they should no longer waste their time with lies." The Midrash comments that this teaches us that they had in their possession *megillos* (scrolls) they used to study on Shabbos. And it was to prevent them from reading these scrolls that Pharaoh increased their labor.

Rabbi Yaakov Kamenetsky posed the question — What became of these *megillos?* — and offered a very interesting solution. The *Gemara* in *Bava Basra* states that Moshe *Rabbeinu* wrote eleven chapters of *Tehillim,* among them *Mizmor Shir LeYom HaShabbos* (Tehillim *92*). Interestingly, the Song for Shabbos does not mention Shabbos at all. Reb Yaakov speculated that it is called *Mizmor Shir LeYom HaShabbos* because it was among those said by the Jews in Egypt on Shabbos. And what is one of the main subjects of that psalm? "[T]the wicked bloom like the grass and all doers of iniquity blossom."

Thus our ancestors, according to Reb Yaakov, spent their Shabbos wondering how Hashem could allow them to suffer so greatly at the hands of the wicked. There in Egypt, they first asked the question of why it so frequently seems that the wicked prosper at the expense of the righteous. Today when we read in the *Haggadah* of "our suffering and affliction and the tremendous pressures on us," we do so as if we were reading *Ashrei*; we do not really feel the affliction of the Jews in Egypt, but they were the first Jews to pose the question of why the righteous suffer.

◄ WHEN HINDSIGHT IS BETTER THAN FORESIGHT

But if the Jewish people during the exile in Egypt first questioned their suffering at the hands of those far more wicked than themselves, it is important to realize that they did find in retrospect explanations for their enslavement because Egypt is the paradigm for all future Jewish suffering. The Torah refers to Egypt as "a crucible for the refining of metal," and indeed it was there that we were purified and prepared for the receipt of the Torah. One of the defining characteristics of the Jewish people is that they are merciful and take pity on the suffering of others. Time after time in the Torah, we are enjoined to treat the stranger, the widow, and the orphan with special consideration "because you were strangers in the land of Egypt."

This concern with the oppressed remains an enduring legacy of Egypt where we were the downtrodden and abused. No matter how assimilated a Jew becomes, as long as he still identifies himself as a Jew he is likely to be found siding with the oppressed. Jews were pioneers in the Civil Rights Movement. It was Jews who marched with blacks in Selma and Montgomery, and it sometimes seems that being Jewish is a prerequisite for working for the American Civil Liberties Union. Whatever the cause, there will always be Jews at the forefront. Much of this idealism is distorted by the lack of Torah guidance, but the concern with society's least fortunate is nevertheless a legacy from Egypt.

Seven days after leaving Egypt, the Sea of Reeds split, and it was about that event that the *Targum Yonasan* comments on the verse, "Israel saw the great Hand that Hashem inflicted upon Egypt" (Shemos 14:31), the departing Jews realized that the experience of Egypt had been a beneficial one for them. The difference was that now they were viewing the situation in retrospect. And so it frequently is in life; only with benefit of hindsight can we appreciate the value of what at the time seemed to be situations of unmitigated pain.

That is the lesson the *Chiddushei HaRim* draws from the order in which we explain the symbols of the *Seder* — Pesach, matzah, and *maror* (the bitter herbs). Logically, he says, *maror,* the symbol of our suffering in Egypt, should come first. But only in light of the Redemption, symbolized by Pesach and matzah, can we understand that suffering, and thus the symbols of Redemption are explained first.

Often with the benefit of hindsight we can begin to see purpose in events that seemed completely incomprehensible at the time. Moshe beseeched Hashem, "Show me now Your glory" (Shemos 33:18), and the *Gemara* in *Berachos* interprets Moshe's request as one for understanding of why the righteous suffer. Hashem responded, "Behold! There is a place near Me; you may stand on the rock. I shall shield you with My hand until I have passed. Then I shall remove My hand and you will see My back, but My face may not be seen" (Shemos 33:22-23).

There is an argument in *Berachos* whether Hashem in fact answered Moshe *Rabbeinu's* question or not. Rabbi Samson Raphael Hirsch, however, learns that the two opinions do not really differ. From the human vantage point, there is no answer to the question. Only from the vantage point of Hashem Himself — for whom all past, present, and future exists at once — can the suffering be explained. That is what Hashem meant when He told Moshe, "There is a place near Me. . ." — only if you could see everything from My perspective above time and space could you understand.

"My back you will see, but My face may not be seen," says the *Chasam Sofer,* refers precisely to the fact that Hashem's ways may sometimes be discerned in retrospect ("My back you will see"), but not prospectively as the events themselves are unfolding ("My face may not be seen").

At the end of every day of the Creation, except the second day, we read, "And G-d saw that it was good." But at the end of Creation "G-d saw all that He had made, and behold it was very good" (Bereishis 1:31). The *Midrash* explains that "good" refers to God's kindness to people; "very good" refers to *midas yissurim* (the afflictions that Hashem brings upon people). In the totality of human history the afflictions visited upon us also have their purpose, but that can only be seen from G-d's perspective encompassing all history from beginning to end; that is why they are alluded to only at the very end of the narrative of Creation.

A parable. Have you ever seen beautiful needlepoints? Some of them are amazing in their intricacy and portray huge tableaus. Yet if one looks at the needlepoint from the opposite side, all one sees is an unsightly, apparently random, mass of threads, knotted and crossed. The reverse side is without apparent logic or beauty. The perspective from which we ask our questions is comparable to that of one who judges the needlepoint from the reverse side. To ask why this string is knotted and this one not is pointless unless we can see the grand design on the other side into which each string fits.

Chassidim tell the story of a chassid who rushed to his rebbe whenever he had troubles. Each time the rebbe prayed for him, and the afflictions soon disappeared. Then the rebbe died and the chassid was left bereft. The first time the chassid found himself in a difficult situation after his rebbe's passing, he had no one to turn to and so hastened to the grave of his rebbe. He begged the rebbe to intervene on his behalf in front of the Heavenly Court, as he had while alive, but this time the chassid's problems were not alleviated.

Shortly thereafter the rebbe came to the chassid in a dream and explained why he had not interceded on his behalf with the Heavenly tribunal. "When I was alive and heard about your various troubles, I felt terrible for you and *davened* that they should be removed. But now that I'm here in Heaven, I see that which we view as troubles on earth are really just the opposite, and I can no longer *daven* for you. It is not that I no longer love you or that I am not concerned with your welfare, but that I now see things from a different vantage point."

Though we have said that often our suffering takes on an entirely different light when we look back at it, the fact remains that very often we have little solace in this world for past pain and die little closer to comprehending a particular tragedy than at the time it occurred. And therefore we continue to ask just as the *navi Yirmiyahu* did: "Why do the wicked prosper?"(Yirmiyahu 1:12). The *navi* Habbakuk gave voice to the same question, and there is an entire book of *Tanach*, Iyov, devoted exclusively to this issue.

✎ WHY BAD THINGS HAPPEN TO GOOD PEOPLE — THE BOOK

More than a decade ago there appeared a book by a Conservative clergyman entitled *Why Bad Things Happen to Good People?* that completely captured the imagination of a public desperate for some answer to the question posed. Rabbi Harold Kushner, the author, was immediately catapulted to fame and came to be viewed as the resident expert on the meaning of human suffering. When the Union Carbide plant in Bhopal, India exploded, poisoning 2,300 people, it was to Rabbi Kushner that National Public Radio turned to put the event in perspective.

Rabbi Kushner's book grew out of a terrible tragedy in his own life, and I want to emphasize that nothing that I may say in criticism of his book should be construed as a lack of sympathy for his and his wife's pain. The Kushners had a bright, three-year-old son named Aaron, who was diagnosed with Rapidly Aging Syndrome, a horrible disease which causes its victims to age a lifetime in six or seven years. The birthdays that are joyous events in the lives of most children mark for a child suffering from this disease another large step closer to death. After the death of his son, Rabbi Kushner undertook an investigation of human suffering. Inevitably, that investigation took him to *Sefer Iyov* (The Book of Job).

As we all know, Iyov was a *tzaddik,* an upright and pure man, of whom Hashem Himself said, "There is not another like him in all the world." Hashem took great delight in His servant, so much so that one day the Satan challenged Him. Iyov, said the Satan, has never been tested, You have favored him with children, friends, and wealth, but who knows how he would fare if tested. Hashem accepted this challenge, and visited upon him the proverbial afflictions of Job. Iyov lost his children, he lost his wealth, and he was afflicted with horrendous sores all over his body.

Iyov had three friends who came to visit him and to console him. They tried to give some explanation for what had befallen him, but all they could offer was that Iyov must not be as great a *tzaddik* as he appeared and his suffering was a Divine punishment. Iyov, however, examined his own soul and could not accept this explanation; he refused to believe that he deserved what had been meted out to him. Next Iyov was visited by Elihu. According to the *Ramban,* Elihu's speeches to Iyov cannot be understood at all on their simplest level. They deal, writes the *Ramban,* with the return of souls in different bodies (*gilgulim)* and other esoteric topics. In the end, Iyov is not comforted by Elihu either.

At last, Hashem Himself speaks to Iyov out of the whirlwind. Hashem surveys with Iyov a wide array of natural phenomena to demonstrate to him how limited is the latter's understanding of their workings. "Where were you when I laid the foundations of the earth? Declare if you have understanding. Who determined its measurements if you know? . . . Where are its foundations fastened?" (Iyov 38:4-6), Hashem challenges Iyov. Over four chapters, there is not one allusion to the problem with which Iyov is struggling: How could a righteous man like himself suffer so horribly? Yet in the end, Iyov is consoled.

Rabbi Kushner attempts to explain what precisely it was that Hashem told Iyov which gave him solace. He concludes that Hashem told Iyov: There is a force in the world called Evil, and this force is beyond My capacity to control. Apparently Rabbi Kushner found it easier to deal with a G-d Who is not omnipotent than one Who could do things that cause people to suffer in ways that are beyond their capacity to understand. He would rather believe in bad luck than a "bad" G-d.

As an interpretation of *Sefer Iyov*, this is, on its face, patently absurd.[1] It is clear that when the Satan visits upon Iyov all his torment, he does so with Hashem's explicit permission, not as an independent, cosmic force of Evil. Moreover, the entire thrust of Hashem's lengthy speech to Iyov is to emphasize the limits of Iyov's understanding — and by extension all human understanding — of the workings of Hashem's world. Rabbi Kushner, however, starts from the assumption that whatever he cannot understand is *ipso facto* unfair, and must be attributed to an evil force beyond Hashem's control.

Most startling of all is that Rabbi Kushner is willing, wittingly or unwittingly, to jettison the most fundamental of all Jewish beliefs — the belief in the absolute unity of Hashem — in order to solve the conundrum of suffering. Hashem's unity is the core of the basic affirmation of Jewish faith — the *Shema* — recited twice daily by every believing Jew. There is religious precedent for his views, but the religion is not Judaism but sixth century Persian Zoroastrianism, which posited a Manichean universe in which the forces of good and evil were in constant conflict.

---

1. Actually, the book's problems begin with the title itself, with its too easy assumption that those who experience bad things are "good people." That title seems to assume that there can be no possible connection between the specific character of the one experiencing the tragedy and the tragedy itself. Traditional Jewish thought, by contrast, insists that the first response to suffering must always be a careful examination of one's actions. We reject, on the one hand, any facile assumption that there is a precise correlation between suffering and one's righteousness or lack thereof. We know that many great *tzaddikim* — indeed the greatest of *tzaddikim* — are among those who suffer terrible tragedies. On the other hand, Jewish thought rejects any conception of that suffering as accidental, i.e., just a matter of bad luck. It may be the very righteousness of the one who suffers that brings about that suffering — for instance, where the suffering is a form of atonement so that Hashem can reward the *tzaddik* with the full measure of reward in the World to Come — but that, too, is specifically related to the character of the one afflicted.

About one thing Rabbi Kushner is surely right. Any search for a Jewish approach to suffering must deal with *Sefer Iyov.* The crucial verse in understanding Iyov's consolation is Iyov's reply to Hashem's speech from out of the whirlwind: "Until now I knew of You through the hearing of the ear, but now my eye sees You" (Iyov 42:5). According to the classical commentators, Iyov contrasts his previous knowledge of Hashem, which was received by tradition, with the prophetic experience he has just had. The prophetic experience of closeness to Hashem has left him indifferent to the timebound concerns of this world and longing to be reunited with Hashem in *Olam Haba.*

Rabbi Moshe Eisemann, author of the ArtScroll *Iyov,* offers a variant of this interpretation. Until Hashem spoke directly to Iyov, Iyov's knowledge of Hashem was purely intellectual. After Hashem took Iyov under His wing for a tour of the cosmos, Iyov experienced an emotional closeness to Hashem in addition to his previous intellectual understanding. Trust is a function of emotional closeness, not intellectual understanding. In the realm of the intellect everything has to fit together. If it does not make sense logically, then you are going to be bothered, just as when you cannot figure out a piece of *Gemara.*

Emotional closeness, however, allows one to live with an intellectual problem because the trust is so great. Take the implicit trust that exists between spouses. Even if one could build an intellectually compelling case that someone's wife had acted to hurt him, he would still reject it out of hand on the grounds that his wife loves him and would never do anything to harm him.

Ibn Ezra expresses a similar thought on the verse, "You are children of HASHEM, Your G-d, you shall not gash yourself [as a sign of mourning]..." (Devarim 14:1). He interprets the verse:

Now that you know that you are children to Hashem,
and that He loves you more than a father loves his son,
do not mutilate yourself over the death of a loved one.
Even if you cannot understand the loss, just as a little
child does not understand the slap on his hand as it
heads for the fire, you must rely on Hashem, just as the
little child continues to rely on the parent who has
slapped him.

That is what happened to Iyov. He became so close to
Hashem and his trust in Hashem was so great that he no longer
needed an answer to his question. Even without being told why
he had been so afflicted, he was consoled.

◄ TURNING TRAGEDY INTO OPPORTUNITY

Sometimes the only way we can deal with a tragedy is by
transforming it into an opportunity, or, as I once heard it said,
by turning fate into destiny. We are dealt a certain hand in life,
and our task is to make the most of it. Or, as a popular poster
put it frivolously, but aptly, "If life deals you a lemon, make
lemonades."

Let me give some examples of what I mean. Every state today
has a chapter of MADD, Mothers Against Drunken Driving, push-
ing state legislatures to curb drunken driving and raise the
teenage drinking age. This organization was started by a mother
whose daughter was killed by a drunken driver, and who translated her individual tragedy into saving other lives. Similarly, the
most effective crusader against the so-called Saturday Night
Special, guns used only to kill and maim people, is Sarah Brady,
wife of James Brady, President Reagan's press secretary, who
was left a paraplegic for life by an assassin's bullet.

For something closer to home, consider the Hebrew Institute for the Deaf founded by Rabbi Moshe Ebstein. Rabbi Ebstein's interest in deaf education was triggered by the fact that two of his sons suffered from deafness. Rather than cursing his fate, Rabbi Ebstein used it as a spur to create an institution that has saved hundreds of Orthodox deaf children who would have been otherwise consigned to the public school system.

I once heard how Rabbi Ebstein developed the strength to transform his personal tragedy into an opportunity. As a young boy during World War II, he was in a Soviet labor camp (this after having escaped from a Nazi concentration camp). He was fortunate in that he was together in the camp with his rebbe. The first Shabbos they realized that if they refused to work, they would be killed on the spot. On the other hand, they could not imagine a Shabbos while working. As the sun set on Friday night, they sang *Lecho Dodi* while still working, and the next morning, they continued with Shabbos *zemiros.* Even as they were *mechalel Shabbos* with their hands, they were sanctifying the Shabbos with their singing. Rabbi Ebstein's rebbe knew the *davening* by heart, as well as the Torah reading. So they *davened* together and recited the Torah reading as they worked that Shabbos and every Shabbos until their release. After more than fifty years, Rabbi Ebstein still remembers those *Shabbosim* as the holiest, the most beautiful of his life. And from that experience in the Soviet labor camp, he learned that there is virtually no situation from which it is not possible to build something beautiful and holy. Doing so is often the only practical therapy for the pain of our misfortunes.

Most of the time when I write or lecture it is in the hope that people will be able to apply the concepts discussed in their everyday lives. It is my hope, however, that these words remain entirely theoretical and that none of us ever need them. May all our tragedies and suffering soon be transformed into cause for rejoicing.

Are We Really Waiting for Mashiach?

We are all preparing for a final exam. There will be only four questions and they will all have simple yes or no answers. Sounds like there should be nothing to worry about. In addition, we are told the questions in advance: Did you conduct your business affairs honestly? Did you set aside time daily for the learning of Torah? Did you occupy yourself with having and raising children? Did you eagerly anticipate the final Redemption? If we can answer all four of these questions affirmatively, we can look forward to a comfortable seat in *Gan Eden.*

With respect to the first three questions at least, it is clear that there has been a lot of preparation for the final exam. In recent years, there have been countless *shmuessen* and conferences devoted to business ethics. The amount of time spent learning far surpasses that of thirty years ago. Not only is yeshiva study *de rigeur* for all sectors of the Orthodox world, but an ever greater percentage of our young men are continuing for many years in *kollel.* Nor is that learning limited to yeshivos and *kollelim,* as the proliferation of Daf Yomi, Dial-a-Daf, Dial-a-Shiur, etc., indicate.

The third question will not be whether you had children, for that is not always in our control, but did you try to have children, and on that score too we would seem to be doing well. As a community, we devote tremendous energy to marrying off our young. No subgroup in America has as many children as religious Jews or makes such great sacrifices to provide a particular type of education to its children.

When we look at these questions, we notice a common thread running through them: They all have to do with our daily lives. The questions do not focus on such yearly events as eating matzah on Pesach or eating in a *succah,* but on our day-to-day activities. The test would seem to be the extent to which our awareness of Hashem permeates every aspect of our diurnal existence.

If it is true that the first three questions all concern our daily activities, then it should be obvious that the anticipation of *Mashiach* — the fourth question — also has to do with our daily thoughts. The longing for *Mashiach* must be part of the very fiber of our beings, not an awareness to which we occasionally arouse ourselves. When we say *Modeh Ani* in the morning, we have to say to ourselves: This could be the day! When no news of *Mashiach's* arrival has reached us by noontime, we should think to ourselves: Already noon, and he still has not come. And as we go to bed, however well the day has gone, there should still be a feeling of something missing: another day without *Mashiach*. I once heard an interview with the wife of someone held captive for six years, and she said, "Not once in the last six years have I gone to bed without thinking that tonight could be the night he is released." And that is precisely how we should think of *Mashiach* as we go to bed.

◄ SOMETHING MISSING

All of us have known what it is to long passionately for something, or at the very least to wait impatiently. Yet despite the fact that we pray three times every day for the coming of *Mashiach*, I doubt many of us could say that we are longing for *Mashiach*, that we feel some absence in our lives that only he can remedy.

In Baltimore, we have only one kosher supermarket, and, as you can imagine, the lines at the checkout counter on *Erev Shabbos* and *Erev Yom Tov* can grow pretty long. People wait in those lines with steam coming out of their ears, as if every moment spent in the line involved the loss of their most precious possession. I once overheard a woman on line remark, "If only we waited for *Mashiach* like we wait for the checkout counter girl to finish with the people in front of us," and I could not help but feel a stab of guilt at how accurate her remark was.

After we had been living for many years on Yeshiva Lane on the Ner Israel campus, the Yeshiva decided to build new townhouses for the *rebbeim*. Ground was broken just after Pesach, and we were assured we would be in our new homes by Rosh Hashanah. By Rosh Hashanah, the end was nowhere in sight, but the builder still promised that we would light our Chanukah menorahs in our new home. With the onset of winter, however, the main water pipe froze and burst. We did not move in until just before Pesach, which at least made Pesach cleaning easy that year.

While our home was being built, I experienced an eager anticipation I had not known since we were waiting for our first baby. It was on my mind constantly. But again, when someone remarked to me, "Now you know what it means to anticipate the Redemption," I felt only pangs of guilt.

Jews did not always have such a hard time looking forward to the coming of *Mashiach*. Jews along the Rhine at the time of the Crusades, or in Spain during the Inquisition, in Poland while Chelminicki's Cossack hordes rampaged or under the Russian Czars knew what it was to wait eagerly for *Mashiach*. For many Jews over the centuries, the coming of *Mashiach* was the only thing to which they could look forward. Our ancestors lived with a *Mashiach* consciousness that we can barely conceive. If one wants any proof of this, just consider the responses to false messiahs like Shabbatei Zvi. At the height of the Shabbatean fervor, whole communities sold their homes and all their assets in preparation for their imminent deliverance. They did not just mouth their belief in the coming of *Mashiach;* they bet, as they say, the house on it.

But what was not a test for our ancestors in Poland and Russia and Germany is a test for those of us fortunate enough to be living among the comforts of America today. In truth, it should be just the opposite. Rabbi Dessler writes in the fourth volume of *Michtav M'Eliyahu* that material affluence is part of the preparation for the advent of *Mashiach*. When our lives no longer need to be focused exclusively on eking out our daily sustenance, we have the peace of mind to direct our attention to spiritual matters and to prepare for a world in which Hashem has revealed Himself for all to see. Yet that affluence is a test. On the one hand, it allows us to direct our thoughts to spiritual matters; on the other hand, it tempts us to an involvement with material luxury, which only coarsens us.

We have been provided an opportunity by Hashem, and we are wasting it. Worse, that opportunity is having exactly the opposite effect from what Hashem intended. The *Shelah Hakodosh* wrote over four hundred years ago, "I see Jews building mansions fit for princes. They build permanent dwellings in this world and in these defiled lands confident that their children and their children's children will inherit them. And this appears as a removal of their thoughts from the Redemption." Those words ring equally true today. We have become entrenched, sure that we are living in a motherland where our grandchildren and great-grandchildren are going to live as well. If *Mashiach* were to come today, our first worry might well be: What am I going to do with the swimming pool?

We are unfortunately like the twelfth grader who told his *rebbe* when the class was studying a *Gemara* about anticipating the ultimate salvation, "If you tell me it's a mitzvah to want *Mashiach* to come, I'll want him. But I really don't need *Mashiach*. I'm learning well. I'm succeeding. Why do I need *Mashiach*?" We suffer from the same problem. We think to ourselves: We're honest; we're *frum; Yiddishkeit* is strong in our city. Who needs *Mashiach*? Since we are no longer in twelfth grade, we know better than to articulate our own lack of longing for *Mashiach*. But when we look deep into our hearts, we know that we could ask the same question as that twelfth-grader.

Rabbi Shimon Schwab gave a beautiful parable for our state of being without *Mashiach,* as well as for our own blithe unawareness of the situation we are in. Imagine you are at a wedding. Everybody is well-dressed, the band is playing, the photographers are snapping away, the smorgasbord is wonderful. Everyone is having a grand time. Only one thing is missing: the bride has not shown up. No matter how attractive the surroundings, most of us realize that a wedding without a bride is nothing. Well, a world without *Mashiach* is a wedding without a bride. Only one difference: We don't even realize that the bride isn't here.

❧ CREATING A SENSE OF ABSENCE

To give an example of the type of longing to which we need to aspire, I would like to share a story about another young boy. This boy was at camp one summer, and try as he might the learning counselor could not stimulate him in any way. The boy just daydreamed the entire summer.

Then one day the *rebbi* was learning a *Gemara* discussing the rebuilding of the *Bais Hamikdash*. Suddenly the boy came alive, as if a bright light had flashed in his head. He was filled with questions. "Do you really mean that the *Bais Hamikdash* is going to be rebuilt and that *Mashiach* could come next year?" he wanted to know. The *rebbi* could not figure out why he had suddenly awakened this dreamy boy from his summer-long lethargy, and so he went to discuss it with the camp director. The director was able to fill in the missing explanation: the boy was an orphan. "He knows," the camp director explained, "that after *Mashiach* comes there will be the revival of the dead, and he will see his parents again." That boy needed *Mashiach* because he needed his parents. He knew that something was missing in his life, and he translated that sense of lacking something into an excitement for *Mashiach*.

For those who think that our lives today could not be any better, a few reminders are in order. The first is that part of the definition of exile is that we can never take our security for granted. As long as the Jew is in exile nothing is for sure. This is not just conjecture but the bitter lesson of the last three thousand years.

The *Gemara* is *Bava Basra* relates a story told by Rabba bar Bar-Chana. Rabba bar Bar-Chana describes a ship voyage in which his boat landed on the back of a whale so huge that he and his fellow sailors mistook it for an island. Sand had even collected on the whale's back. Thinking the whale was an island, Rabba bar Bar-Chana and his companions disembarked and made a fire on the back of the whale to cook and bake. Eventually the whale noticed the fire on its back and to remove the burning sensation flipped over entirely. Had Rabba bar Bar-Chana and his companions not succeeded in laying hold of their nearby boat, they would have drowned.

The *Maharshah* explains the symbolism of the Rabba bar Bar-Chana's tale. The sea is the historical voyage of the Jewish people throughout exile. The back of the whale is the various different lands in which we sought refuge and over the course of time began to think of as our homes. And there we baked and cooked — i.e., we put down roots and raised families. But eventually the whale turned over to rid itself of the Jews on its back, just as the nations in which we found sanctuary eventually expelled us or permitted the rabble to murder us in the thousands and millions. Whether it was Spain in 1492 or Kiev in 1648 or Germany in 1940, the whale has turned over again and again.

Just when we were beginning to think that America would prove the exception to the general rule, Crown Heights erupted and we saw how easily the Jew could become the scapegoat for all the nation's pent-up racial tensions. And a former member of the American Nazi Party and grand wizard of the Klu Klux Klan forced a run-off in his campaign for governor of Louisiana.

My wife and I took a summer vacation to Toronto a few years ago and we decided to take a bus tour of the city. Sitting behind us on the bus were two elderly British gentlemen with lovely British accents. I would never have picked them out as Jewish, but when I approached them at one of the stops, they shocked me by greeting me, "*Shalom Aleichem.*"

These were two assimilated Jews from Manchester, and yet their first question to me was: Is there much anti-Semitism in

Baltimore? I was shocked by the question because I have never felt much anti-Semitism at all. But a few weeks later, I received a letter from a former student studying in Manchester, in which he wrote that the lurking anti-Semitism in Europe is palpable. Traveling in what we think of as the world's most civilized countries — Belgium, France, and Italy — one feels it all the time.

We may not feel it in America, but that is an illusion. Who do you think will be among the first targets of the proliferating paramilitary groups like the one responsible for the Oklahoma City bombing. Rabbi Berel Wein points out that the Jews are the only victims of mass horror and genocide who go around chanting talismanically, "Never Again." The very fact that there is such a slogan shows that we know deep down it *can* happen again.

The point is not to scare ourselves into waiting as we should for *Mashiach,* but to appreciate that our situation, as ever, is a very tenuous one. Even observed objectively, there is no reason for us to be sanguine about the state of *Yiddishkeit* in America. We may have our Dial-a-Daf and *chalav Yisrael,* fine yeshivos and Bais Yaakovs for our children, and a son-in-law or two in Lakewood, but the general situation in *Klal Yisrael* is tragic. Since 1985, 52% of Jews marrying have married non-Jews. And in such marriages, 41% of the children are raised in some other faith and 31% with no religion at all. Of the remaining 28%, who knows how many of the offspring are even *halachically* Jewish, and one does not have to guess too much about the quality of their "Jewish education." In Israel, the rise of satanic cults, numerous killings and assaults in pubs catering almost exclusively to teenagers, and the murder of a taxi driver "for the fun of it" by two 15-year-olds from an affluent suburb have provoked calls for more religious instruction, even from the devoutly secular.

In such a situation, we cannot afford to say, "*Shalom al nafshi* — Everything is alright with me." We talk about *Klal*

Yisrael, the Jewish people, as being one collective body, with our fellow Jews as other limbs on that body, but we do not really believe it, or at least do not act as if we believe it. If we did, we would feel a lot less comfortable in America today.

We must avoid the feeling that we will take care of ours and let the non-religious take care of theirs. When we drink a second, better wine at the table, we make the blessing *hatov ve'hamativ* "to the One Who is good and does good." This *berachah* was originally formulated by *Chazal* and in expanded form made part of *Bircas HaMazon* as a remembrance of the fact that the bodies of those killed at Betar did not decompose and smell prior to burial, despite a years-long delay in burial. Rabbi Yehonsan Eibeshutz in his *Ya'aros Devash* explains the connection between the second bottle of wine and *hatov ve'hamativ.* Betar was a community that felt it could survive, whatever the situation of the rest of *Klal Yisrael.* Its inhabitants rejoiced in their glory oblivious to the destruction of Jerusalem. And that is why we remember them precisely when things are going well with us, when we have a surfeit of wine and the other delicacies that gladden a man's heart. At precisely that moment we are commanded to remember the rest of *Klal Yisrael,* to remember the hundreds of thousands of Jews who cannot even read Hebrew. Today young Jews are more familiar with sushi than matzah balls. A generation ago we at least had gastronomic Jews. Today we do not even have that.

Nor is all so well with us even within our protected enclaves. We are living in a sick environment, and just as pollution does not recognize political boundaries so too moral pollution will not stop at the edge of our neighborhoods. What would have been considered pornography fifteen years ago is today a legitimate advertisement in *The New York Times.* During the hearings over Clarence Thomas' nomination to the Supreme Court and in discussions of the president's alleged infidelities the media has been filled with lurid discussions of matters that once could not have been discussed in public. Even more than in the time of the *Shelah Hakodosh,* we are living in defiled, impure lands. And it is becoming increasingly difficult to isolate ourselves from the impurity all around.

But everything that I have mentioned until now as missing from our lives is really secondary. The most important thing we are missing in our lives is *Mashiach* himself. True, he will remedy all the other problems we have been discussing — the physical insecurity of the Jewish people both outside of *Eretz Yisrael* and in *Eretz Yisrael,* the ignorance of the vast majority of the world's Jews of the rudiments of their heritage, the moral pollution that characterizes the modern world. But those are only symptoms of Hashem's hiddenness from us, His failure to reveal His glory to the entire world. We pray over and over again during Rosh Hashanah and Yom Kippur, "Reign over the entire universe in Your glory... Let everything that you have made know that You are its Creator." Until that takes place, we are living truncated, impoverished lives.

The Divine Presence is in exile, and for that Jews used to rise in the middle of the night and pour out their tears in *Tikkun Chatzos.* And if we really felt the poverty of our lives, how far our world is from the one for which we yearn, we would do so as well.

As long as our lives are going well and we are not immediately touched by tragedy, everything is well with us. But when tragedy strikes us personally or in our community, we realize how opaque the world really is. We ask why, but can receive no answers. Why are children killed in car accidents and young mothers and fathers, *Rachmana l'tzlan,* taken in the prime of life? We go to the eulogies and to the community gatherings called to arouse us to *teshuvah* and introspection, but no one can tell us what we must do. We live in a world in which Hashem has hidden his face. If the Divine Presence were not in exile along with us, there would be prophets who could tell us what to do and why these tragedies occur. But we have neither the *Kohen Gadol* with the *Urim V'Tumim* nor the prophets. So we speculate as to the meaning of events, but we can never know.

After I spoke once on this subject, I received a letter from a woman, who captured beautifully this feeling of being lost:

> *Last year, at exactly this time, we gave birth to a little girl. We were delighted because she was our seventh child and preceded by many brothers. Within hours of her birth, however, we discovered that the right side of her heart had not formed properly and she would need immediate open heart surgery. After three and a half months of struggling, our daughter released her tenuous hold on life and returned to Hashem.*
>
> *Your words were particularly poignant for me because throughout our daughter's illness, we sought advice from various religious people. Some told us that this had happened because we were bad. Some breathed heavily and looked very sad. And one man said, as you did last night, that we have no way of truly knowing why, because Hashem is behind a cloud and we have no prophet to ask for a definitive reason.*
>
> *Because of these difficult circumstances, I pray daily with great fervor for Mashiach to come and honestly expected him hourly. Our tragedy has made us very aware of our need for Mashiach.*

◄ THE SIGNS ARE THERE

All the greatest Torah authorities are in agreement — and have been for at least half a century — that we are today living in the era preceding the coming of *Mashiach*. How long that will last no one knows, but we are in the final stages. The signs are there for anyone with eyes to see. One of the telltale indications of the coming of *Mashiach* is the ingathering of Jews from all parts of the world. In the past five years, we have witnessed hundreds of thousands of Jews from the Soviet Union, who were thought to be irretrievably lost, arriving in *Eretz Yisrael*. So too have the last of the Jews who lived in Yemen for over two millennia and who preserved their Judaism intact.

The last of the prophets, Malachi, described the pre-Messianic era as one in which children will return the hearts of their fathers to Hashem. For thousands of years, Jews have learned that verse in Malachi and not really been sure what the prophet meant. Only now with the growth of the *ba'al teshu-vah* movement over the last twenty years do we know. And this is perhaps the greatest harbinger of *Mashiach*.

A fully secular woman in Israel moved near the outskirts of Bnei Brak. Because she was a fearful, overprotective mother, she did not want her daughter traveling by bus to school, and so she enrolled her in a religious school near their home. The daughter started becoming more and more religious. One Friday, she begged her mother to let her light Shabbos candles, which her mother forcefully refused to allow her to do. Finally, the little girl ran to the nearby grocer and asked him for Shabbos candles. Knowing that the family was not religious, the grocer thought she must want *yahrzeit* candles. That night, when the little girl did not appear for dinner, her parents went up to her room. They opened the door and found her standing in front of two *yahrzeit* candles. The little girl explained innocently to her parents, "One is for Abba (father) and one is for Imma (mother)." The sight of her own *yahrzeit* candle shocked her mother very deeply. She realized, without knowing the *Chazal,* that even in life she was already dead and she became a *ba'alas teshuvah.*

These are the times we live in — the ingathering of the exiles, children bringing their parents back to Hashem. The footsteps of *Mashiach, ikvesa d'mashicha,* are heard.

✒ WHAT CAN WE DO?

My friend Rabbi Paysach Krohn once told me something very interesting about the blessing in *Shemoneh Esrei* in which we pray for the reestablishment of the Davidic dynasty with the coming of *Mashiach.* When we pray for forgiveness, we close our supplication "for *You* grant forgiveness." Similarly, when we pray for health, we conclude, "for *You* are G-d, King, a faithful and merciful healer." But in this blessing, we do not conclude, "for You are a G-d Who brings *Mashiach,*" but rather "because for Your salvation *we* hope all the day."

The coming of *Mashiach* is not just dependent on Hashem but on us, on the extent to which we hope for him all the day, every day. And if he has still not come, the reason perhaps is that we do not in fact hope for him "all the day" as we profess to.

Prior to becoming the *rav* in Brisk, the *Bais Halevi,* Rabbi Yosef Ber Soloveitchik, was the *rav* in another town. His experience as *rav* was not a happy one and he determined never to become a *rav* again. When a delegation from Brisk approached him to offer him the *rabbonus* of Brisk, the jewel of Lithuanian Jewry, he refused on the grounds that he was retired from the rabbinate. One of the members of the delegation from Brisk however was not so easily put off. "There are twenty thousand Jews in Brisk waiting for you to become *rav,*" he said. "How can you refuse?" The *Bais Halevi* had no answer and agreed to become the *rav* of Brisk.

When the *Chafetz Chaim* heard this story, he cried. Do we imagine that *Mashiach* is less sensitive than the *Bais Halevi.*

Are We Really Waiting for Mashiach? □ 249

And if the *Bais Halevi* felt he could not deny twenty thousand Jews, how can *Mashiach* deny millions who pray for his coming? The answer, the *Chafetz Chaim* concluded, is that there are not twenty thousand Jews really waiting for *Mashiach*. And that is what we have to change.

NOTES

NOTES

NOTES

NOTES

NOTES

This volume is part of
THE ARTSCROLLSERIES®
an ongoing project of
translations, commentaries and expositions
on Scripture, Mishnah, Talmud, Halachah,
liturgy, history, the classic Rabbinic writings,
biographies, and thought.

For a brochure of current publications
visit your local Hebrew bookseller
or contact the publisher:

Mesorah Publications, ltd

4401 Second Avenue
Brooklyn, New York 11232
(718) 921-9000